The Identity of Hispanoamerica

THE IDENTITY
OF HISPANOAMERICA

An Interpretation of Colonial Literature

José Promis

Translated from the Spanish by Alita Kelley and Alec E. Kelley

The University of Arizona Press   Tucson

The University of Arizona Press
Copyright © 1991
The Arizona Board of Regents
All Rights Reserved

A revised and amplified version of a work originally published as *La identidad de Hispanoamérica: Ensayo sobre literatura colonial* by the Universidad de Guadalajara.

♾ This book is printed on acid-free, archival-quality paper.

96 95 94 93 92 91   6 5 4 3 2 1

Library of Congress Cataloging-in-Publication Data

Promis Ojeda, José.
    [Identidad de hispanoamérica. English]
    The identity of Hispanoamerica : an interpretation of colonial
literature / José Promis ; translated from the Spanish by Alita
Kelley and Alec E. Kelley.
        p. cm.
    Rev. translation of La identidad de hispanoamérica.
    Includes bibliographical references and index.
    ISBN 0-8165-1251-5 (cloth)
    1. Spanish American literature—To 1800—History and criticism.
2. Literature and society—Latin America.   3. Latin America—
Intellectual life.   I. Title.
PQ7081.P7613   1991
860.9'98—dc20   91-9979
                                                           CIP

British Library Cataloguing in Publication data are available.

CONTENTS

AUTHOR'S PREFACE

The original version of *La identidad de Hispanoamérica* published by the University of Guadalajara in 1987 was addressed to readers of Spanish familiar with the literature and culture of colonial Hispanic America. For this reason, the text contained suggestions, allusions, and some historical data, all of which would be perfectly comprehensible to the intended reader. The present version in English does not assume that readers have such knowledge but hopes rather to awaken an interest in Hispanoamerican culture and literature. Consequently, it is not a literal translation of the original *La identidad de Hispanoamérica* but a somewhat revised, corrected, and expanded version of that text written with readers of English in mind. For all the sources quoted, both poetry and prose, the translators attempted to keep as close in meaning as possible to the Spanish originals, while producing a result that would be appropriate in English and yet retain the flavor of the period.

I should like to express my appreciation to Celestino Fernández, associate vice president for academic affairs, and Norman Austin, dean of the Faculty of Humanities of the University of Arizona for arranging financial support for the publication of this text. Special thanks to Dr. Karl C. Gregg for checking and correcting the translations of the quoted poetic texts. Above all, however, my thanks to Professor Charles A. Tatum, head of the Department of Spanish and Portuguese of the University of Arizona; his enthusiasm and confidence in the original text formed the starting point for this translation, and his active participation in the project made this publication possible.

CHRONOLOGY OF LITERATURE AND EVENTS

Literature in Spain	Historical Events	Literature in Spanish America
Anon., *Poema de mío Cid* (ca. 1140)		
Don Juan Manuel (1282–1340), *Libro de Conde Lucanor* *Libro de los Estados*		
Juan Ruiz (ca. 1283–1350), *Libro de Buen Amor* (ca. 1330)		
Marquis de Santillana (1398–1458), *serranillas*		
Jorge Manrique (ca. 1440–79), *Coplas a la muerte de su padre* (1476)		Columbus (1451–1506), *Commentaries; Diary; Letters*
Antonio Nebrija [Lebrixa] (ca. 1441–1552), *Castillian Grammar* (1492)	1474, Ferdinand and Isabella reign over united Spain	Juan Ponce de León (ca. 1460–1521)
	1492, conquest of Granada; discovery of America	
Peter Mártir (ca. 1455–1510), *New World Decades* (1494–1510)		
Anon., *La Celestina* (ca. 1499)		
Garci-Rodríguez (Garci-Ordoñez) de Montalvo, *Amadís de Gaul* (1508)	1504, death of Queen Isabella	
	1516, death of King Ferdinand	
	1517, Charles I, King of Spain; Luther publishes his theses	Hernán Cortés (1485–1547), *Letters to Charles V* (1519–26)
	1519, Charles becomes king of Austria	Gonzalo F. de Oviedo (1478–1557), *Historia general* (1526–49)
	1519–22, conquest of Mexico	
	1521, Charles becomes Charles V, Holy Roman emperor	Alvar Nuñez Cabeza de Vaca (ca. 1490–ca. 1559)
Juan Luis Vives (1492–1540), *Instruction of the Christian Woman* (1524)		
Garcilaso de la Vega (ca. 1502–36), *poems*		Bartolomé de Las Casas (1474–1566), *Apologética historia* (1527)
Hernando de Acuña (ca. 1520–ca. 1585), *Sonnet to the King*	1531–35, conquest of Peru	*Brevísima relación* (1552) *Historia de las Indias* (1527–61)
	1545–63, Council of Trent	Pedro de Valdivia (1500–53), *Letters to Charles V* (1545–50)
Anon., *Lazarillo de Tormes* (1553)		
	1556, Charles V abdicates; Philip II, king of Spain	Bernal Díaz del Castillo (1495–1584),
	1580, Philip II annexes Portugal	*True History* (ca. 1580–83)

Literature in Spain	Historical Events	Literature in Spanish America
		Francisco de Terrazas (ca. 1525–ca. 1600), *sonnets*
Luis de León (1527–91), *De los nombres de Cristo* (ca. 1585)		Alonso de Ercilla (1533–94), *La Araucana* (1569, 1578, 1589)
	1588, defeat of the Spanish Armada	Juan Suárez de Peralta (ca. 1540–ca. 1590), *Discovery of the Indies* (1589)
	1598, death of Philip II	José de Acosta (1540–1600), *Historia natural y moral* (1590)
Mateo Alemán (1546–1614), *Guzman de Alfarache* (1599)		Inca Garcilasco de la Vega (1539–1616), *Comentarios reales* (1609)
Miguel de Cervantes (1547–1616), *Don Quixote* (1605, 1615)		Bernardo de Balbuena (ca. 1561–1627), *Siglo de oro* (before 1592, pub. 1608)
Luis de Góngora (1561–1627), *poems*		*El Bernardo* (1592, pub. 1624) *Grandeza mexicana* (1602, pub. 1604)
Félix Lope de Vega Carpio (1562–1635), *sonnet, plays*		
Rodrigo Caro (1573–1647), *To the Ruins of Itálica*		Pedro de Oña (1570–ca. 1643), *Arauco domado* (1596) *St. Ignatius of Cantabria* (1639)
	1621, death of Philip III	
Francisco de Quevedo (1580–1665), *poems* *Vida del buscón* (1626)		Diego de Hojeda (1571–1615), *La cristiada* (1611)
		Francisco Bramón (?–1654), *Los sigueros de la Virgen* (1620)
		Juan Rodríguez Freile (1566–ca. 1640), *El carnero* (1636)
		Juan Ruiz de Alarcón (1580–1639), *plays*
	1640, Portugal gains independence	Juan de Palafox (1600–1659), *El pastor de Nochebuena* (1644)
		Miguel de Guevara (ca. 1585–ca. 1646), *sonnets*
Pedro Calderón de la Barca (1600–81), *La vida es sueño*		
		Juan de Ayllón (ca. 1604–?), *23 Martyrs of Japan* (1630)
		Alonso de Ovalle (1601–51), *Histórica relación* (1646)

Literature in Spain	Historical Events	Literature in Spanish America
		Hernando Domínguez Camargo (1606–59), *St. Ignatius Loyola* (1666) *poems* (1676)
	1665, death of Philip IV	Francisco Núñez de Pineda (1607–82), *El cautivero feliz* (1656–73)
		Matías de Bocanegra (1612–68), *Canción*
		Juan de Espinosa Medrano (1632–88), *Apology for Góngora* (1662)
		Sor Juana Inés de la Cruz (1648–95), *Letter to Sor Filotea* (1691) *poems* *Primero sueño*
		Carlos Sigüenza y Góngora (1645–1700), *Infortunios* (1690)
		Juan del Valle Caviedes (ca. 1652–ca. 1698), *Diente de Parnaso* *Sonnet*
	1700, death of Charles III	
		Manuel Lacunza (1731–1801), *La venida del Mesías* (1790)

INTRODUCTION

Hispanoamerican intellectual thought arose from a concept of reality that the Spanish brought to the New World—a dynamic response built on a European foundation and modified, permanently, so that it differs from the one left behind in the country of origin. The *criollos* (this term generally denotes not only persons of Spanish descent born here but also Spaniards who settled on American soil), who began the Hispanoamerican literary process, upheld the norms in force in the far away Iberian Peninsula; they understood the concept and function of *literature* or of *the written word in general* in a way similar to that currently in force in Spain and used the same structures and motifs found in Peninsular literature of the time. Similarity, however, should not be confused with simple imitation, nor should it be thought that an intellectual process originating in Spain continued quite naturally in the newly discovered lands of America. From its beginnings writing in the New World made its own mark and arose not so much from the structures used as from the view of life and the attitudes projected on common elements by Hispanoamerican *criollo* writers, whether native- or Spanish-born.

From its very beginnings Hispanoamerican intellectual thought took the form of a synthesis expressing a new awareness of life itself and of the code that came into being when unknown realities had to be faced; literary work produced by such a synthesis is, in its very nature, dialectic. The same intrinsic nature of literary work produced by such circumstances originates, indeed demands, its own idiosyncratic mode of expression, and this is the one for which the Cuban writer Alejo Carpentier (1904–80) coined the name (with obvious affinities to the term "Third World") the "Third Style of America."

While the more culturally developed pre-Columbian areas already had their own distinctive forms of creative expression when the Spanish arrived here, these were submerged by the intellectual hegemony of the empire and have come down to us as ancillary documents of an almost anthropological nature. These words of the conquered, expressed as they are in a language strange in its idiosyncracies, and in spite of their scarcity amounting to almost complete disappearance, have, nevertheless, left a characteristic imprint on some forms of cultural expression.

This study concentrates on the development and transformation of the dominant tendencies, on the way in which thought arrived from Spain and took root in the soil of the New World, generating a spirit which marks the birth of Hispanoamerica as a historical reality. From the very beginning Hispanoamerican awareness is revealed as alert, polemical, critical, and self-reviewing, consequently subject to doubt, instability, uneasiness, and sudden fears. Hispanoamerican intellectual malaise is a risk, perhaps a weakness, but it offers a never-to-be-abandoned expectation for change and for hope.

The Identity of Hispanoamerica

CHAPTER 1
THE THRESHOLD OF MODERN AWARENESS

THE MEDIEVAL "GOOD HOUSE"

Ancient maps make very clear the exact limits between the real world and the unknown and fantastic, between the space dominated by human presence and a circumference of enigmas extending toward the infinite: "Here there be monsters." To cross the line drawn by the cartographer meant facing uncontrollable unknown forces, which sometimes inspired wonderful worlds of the imagination, but more often, in the experience of the immediate, concrete, historic moment, provoked suspicion and wariness, if not downright terror. In the centuries before Columbus, European imagination found protection and security only when reality was enclosed within established frontiers, within spaces bearing familiar names and a familiar atmosphere. Either a silent void or fantastical beasts probably awaited those adventurers who dared go beyond the limits, who dared leave home—the place where everything belonged, had its proper housing, and obeyed an established, peaceful order.

About 1330 Juan Ruiz (ca. 1283–1350), archpriest of Hita, in Castile, wrote, while imprisoned, one of the most important books of medieval Spain, *Libro de buen amor* [Book of Good Love], in which the author aims at showing the dangers of profane love and the pleasures and rewards that can come only from the love acceptable to God—that is, the love of God's own divinity. The text begins by addressing Our Lord, reminding him of the many times he had "saved" notable persons in the course of history—among them, Jonah, who, after spending three days in the belly of a whale, was taken from there "just as if he had *come out of a good house*" [Spanish version as edited by Anthony N. Zahareas in *The Book of True Love*, Pennsylvania State University Press, 1978]:

Señor Dios, que a los jodíos, pueblo de perdiçión,
sacaste de cabtivo del poder de Farón;
a Daniel sacaste del poço de Babilón,
¡saca a mí coitado desta mala presión!

Señor, tú diste graçia a Ester la reína;
antel el rey Asuero ovo tu graçia digna;
Señor, dame tu graçia e tu merçed aína,
¡sácame desta lazeria, desta presión!

Señor, tú que sacaste al profecta del lago,
de poder de gentiles sacaste a Santiago,
a Santa Marina libreste del vientre del drago,
libra a mí, Dios mío, desta presión do yago.

Señor, tú que libreste a Santa Susaña
del falso testimonio de la falsa conpaña,
líbrame, mi Dios, desta coita tan maña,
dame tu misericordia, tira de mí tu saña.

A Jonás el profecta del vientre de la ballena,
en que moró tres días dentro en la mar llena,
sacástelo tú sano, así como de casa buena,
¡Mexías, tú me salva sin culpa e sin pena!

Señor, a los tres niños de muerte los libraste,
del forno del grand fuego sin lisión [saqueste];
de las ondas del mar a Sant Pedro tomeste;
¡Señor, de aquesta coita saca al tu arçipreste!

Aún tú, que dixiste a los tus servidores
que con ellos serías ante reys dezidores,
e les dirás palabras que fabrasen mejores;
¡Señor, tú sey comigo, guárdame de traidores!

Lord God, who saved the Jews (a damnèd folk)
from captivity under Pharaoh's power,
who saved Daniel from the pit in Babylon,
take me quickly from this evil prison!

Lord, Thou gavest grace to Esther, the Queen;
before King Ahasuerus she had Thy worthy grace;
Lord, give me Thy grace and mercy most soon,
save me from this torment, from this prison!

Lord, who didst take the prophet from the pit,
save Saint James from the infidels,
and free Saint Marina from the dragon's belly;
free me, my God, from this prison where I lie.

Lord, Thou didst release Holy Susannah
from false witness given by false company;
free me, my God, from this evil custom,
grant me Thy mercy, take from me Thy wrath.

Jonah, the prophet, from the belly of the whale
in which three days he dwelt and in the sea,
Thou broughtest safely *as from out a good house*;
Messiah, save Thou me without guilt and sorrow!

Lord, Thou did'st preserve three youths from death,
unharmed, from the great fiery furnace;
did'st raise Saint Peter from waves of the sea;
Lord, from this care pray take Thy priest.

Although Thou hast unto Thy servants said
that, speaking with kings, Thou would'st be with them
and give them words to speak more eloquent;
Lord, be with me and save me from betrayers.

This idea of *la casa buena* (the good house, or good home) should
not be thought of as a felicitous expression originating with the poet
Juan Ruiz; it is not an isolated poetic image in his medieval literary
text, but rather a constantly recurring implied metaphor born of the
cosmic awareness typical of the medieval mind and found in literary
texts of the age prior to the discovery of America.

In general terms, medieval writing constructed its reality on the
solid foundations of an immediate and known cosmic home: up above
is the supernatural level, the realm of God; down below the dark king-

dom of Satan; in between is human space, a transitional testing place. God is the architect who designed man's home, establishing its order and meaning from the beginning of time. As Victor Frankl has pointed out, one of the clearest expressions of this concept is found in St. Augustine's *City of God* (413–426), when he says "God has determined the order of times and terms of habitation of each village so that they might search for Him." This search is the guiding force, the mover, and at the same time the final destination of all movement, no matter how great the distance which lies, or comes to exist, between travelers and their starting points. Displacement always takes place only within the space of the good house which God has given to humankind, and the limits are clearly pointed out by the protecting finger of the Church. So long as a person maintains a link to the divine, a permanent contact with the creator, the space traveled in will always be a familiar one, an enclosure offering protection and security. The enemy forces of the unknown withdraw, pushed back by the roof of the heavenly home, which, like a snail shell or divine umbrella, is always along to cover the head of one who walks with God.

With the exhausting of medieval concepts, the cosmic image of the good house began to weaken too. The *Libro de buen amor* is, in this sense, the meeting point; within it the home-loving spirit of the medieval period and the new intellectual code that desanctifies the forms of established awareness converge and crystallize. Juan Ruiz is one of the first imaginary travelers who, moved by the human curiosity to know, dares to step into the prohibited space. His daring, however, ends in fear and trembling. Sections of the text deal with the poet's meetings with a series of women whom he stumbles upon when he goes out to investigate the surroundings of Hita. The last of these, the girl from the hills near Tablada, is a virago who threatens to break every bone in his body if he will not do as she asks. After this shattering experience, Juan Ruiz returns, contrite and praising God, to the home he had left. His daring escape into the external world ends in the chapel of Santa María del Vado, and his modern-type literary adventure closes in the medieval manner with a vigil and a canticle in honor of the Virgin Mary.

The final crossing of the threshold of the "good home" to reach an outside freedom came at last in the poems known as *serranillas* (mountain songs) by Iñigo López de Mendoza, Marqués de Santillana (1398–1458). These are late medieval poems of gallantry in the *pastour-*

elle tradition in which a nobleman tries, often successfully, to win the favors of one shepherdess or another. These texts reveal feudalism in decline, and the nobleman is, in fact, only exercising his rights over the mountain girls according to the social structure of the time. Nevertheless, the *serranillas* show that a new renaissance outlook has reached Spain. In most of the compositions the motif is that of the journey or quest, but, unlike Juan Ruiz's frustrated excursion, one of the characteristic traits in Santillana's work is the satisfactory amorous culmination of the journey. Such an erotic reward is available to one who dares leave home and venture into the unknown world outside. Exterior space no longer has the negative connotations shown in the imagination of the high Middle Ages; on the contrary, it has become a place for human potential, an opportunity to make real the secret curiosities previously hidden beneath the rigid official ideological schema of the period.

In Santillana the journey (by means of the written word) is no longer a displacement toward the world above, toward the mythic meeting with God of Christian imagery—the only intellectual movement permitted to the inhabitants of the good house. The Christian heaven has been secularized and turned into the garden of earthly delights; man's journey through the world ends in an imaginary feast of the senses.

Venturing out was still forbidden in the literary space contained in the *Libro de buen amor*. In Santillana's *serranillas*, however, the concept of *limits* has disappeared, and in their place the poet's vision discovers, to his surprise, that the journey is a privileged form of human endeavor and at the end of the road there are neither monsters nor punishment. Instead, marvelous personages and unsuspected satisfactions await the appetites of the traveler.

HOME IN THE NEW WORLD

As the concept of the "good house" weakened in Spanish literature, it emerged again in the form of a new home in America. At the same time, the work known as *La Celestina* or *The Tragicomedy of Calixto and Melibea*, written in Spain about 1499, shows the original home losing its protective characteristics; it is becoming a realm which harbors alien passions and conduct that goes against the current social code. At approximately the same time the first texts about Hispanoamerica show that the medieval "good house" has been rebuilt there, in spite of the renaissance intellectual landscape surrounding it. America is revealed to the eyes of the astonished conquistadors as a doubly blessed utopia: a dream come true and a place in which to recapture a lost cosmic ideal. In word and deed—the deed being domination of a new land, the word being imaginative and written—the conquistadors try to rebuild the "good house" left behind across the ocean.

It has often been said that the first sight of America was as if it were in a dream. There is also a school of thought holding that the conquistadors, on reaching the West Indies, forgot their past completely and were as if reborn to a totally new and different life. Both interpretations, while valid enough, fail to give a complete picture, since the first image of America arises from a dialectic vision of utopian possibilities from the perspective of home from which the New World was viewed. This way of seeing reality started with Columbus (1451–1506) himself: the admiral extols the wonders of the newfound lands, and at the same time stresses their continuance with the distant European world. When, for example, he talks of the natives who came to visit him, he mentions that their skins are the color of Canary Islanders'. On the island he visited on October 14, there are "orchards as fine and leafy as any I've seen in Castile in April and May." On Fernandina Island, in spite of the trees being very different from those back in Spain, they are still "as green and lavish as in May in Andalucia." His analogies lead him, in fact, to assert that "there were nightingales and a thousand other little birds singing even though it was November."

Naturally, the first observers of the New World had no basis for comparison other than their own personal experience; nevertheless, the way in which they speak of the New World gives rise to its being seen as the good home refound, thus preparing the way for imperial conquest, as a right to be exercised over a place already its own and not the subjugation of alien territory. The same year as the discovery of America, the fall of Granada successfully concluded the Christian reconquest of Spain, and the two totally separate events held between them secret cosmic relations for the medieval mind of the time.

Columbus's comments are the first to reveal the perspective with which the early chroniclers of the Indies will look at the New World. The concrete reality of the continent is turned into an intellectual concept born of a confrontation, either explicit or implicit, between the Peninsular mind and that world. Nothing better illustrates the cosmic linearity of the early attitude when faced with the reality of America than the amazed description of Tenochtitlán by Hernán Cortés (1485–1547). Cortés, who headed the conquest of the Aztec empire, describes their capital in the letter he sent to the king of Spain in 1520. Charles, the grandson of Ferdinand and Isabella, had become King Charles I of Spain in 1517, but following his election as Holy Roman Emperor as Charles V in 1521 is generally referred to by the more grandiose title. In spite of the incredible diversity of objects, like a world of marvels spread before the conquistadors, or, perhaps for that very reason, Cortés tried to establish a connection between that world and the one he knew in Spain, between the newly discovered and that which was familiar, going from initial astonishment to calming comparisons, such as the one quoted by Alfonso Reyes in his *Visión de Anáhuac, 1519* [First View of Anáhuac, 1519] (1917): the Aztec maguey syrup is "much better than *arrope*" (a confection made by boiling down honey or wine).

This way of describing the new made it easily pictured by everyone in Europe: apart from the things that are *really* different, America is just an enormous place that fits into the medieval good house by the will of the Almighty; those rules which govern human behavior apply too in the newly discovered lands. America enters history as a glorious, shining example of the divine design that orders the known and pushes humanity ever forward into the unknown with the future foreordained.

In the minds of the first intellectuals to write about America, Columbus's epic journey was not seen as an episode breaking the supernatural rhythm of history, but as irrefutable proof of its permanence and continuity. Spatially, the New World blends into the medieval home and so avoids seeming alien and outlandish; America is made to appear as peaceful as home, and to harmonize and be assimilated into it.

The most famous chronicler of the West Indies in Europe during the sixteenth century, Fray Bartolomé de Las Casas (1474–1566) proposes two criteria for understanding the discovery of America. According to Fray Bartolomé it is human nature to go forth and discover unknown lands, to seek to find out what is not known—these are needs that "by nature move appetites, which, having left their homelands, become pilgrims in other lands." This, however, is not a matter of the individual's will nor entirely to that person's credit, but rather is a result of Fray Bartolomé's second factor: the divine plan for guiding historic events:

pero más con verdad creer y afirmar convendrá que Aquél que formó y
crió el universo, que con suavidad todas las cosas criadas gobierna y
dispone, y todo para utilidad y salud del fin por quien todas las hizo,
que es el hombre, con el cuidado que con su universal providencia de su
perfección, no solamente en lo que toca al espíritu, pero aun a lo que
concierne a lo humano y temporal, siempre tiene, levanta e inclina, y
despierta los corazones a que pongan en obra lo que él para la nobilí-
sima y suma perfección y total hermosura de la universalidad de las
criaturas (que en la diferencia y variedad y compostura y orden de sus
repartidas bondades consiste), tiene, desde antes que hubiese siglos, en
su mente divina proveído; y porque los hombres, como no sean la más
vil parte del Universo, antes nobilísimas criaturas y para quien toda
(como se ha tocado) la otra máquina mundial ordenó, por una especial
y más excelente manera de la divinal Providencia, y, si se puede sufrir
decirse, de principal intento sean dirigidos a su fin, y para hincha-
miento y perfecta medida del número de los escogidos, población copiosa
de aquella santa ciudad y moradas eternas, reino con firmeza seguro de
todas las gentes y de todas las lenguas y de todos los lugares, los ciuda-
danos della se hayan de coger, ni antes mucho tiempo, ni después
muchos años, sino el día y la hora que desde antes que algo criase, con
infalible consejo y con justo juicio lo tiene dispuesto; entonces se saben
y entonces parecen y entonces las ocultas naciones son descubiertas y
son sabidas, cuando es ya llegado, cuando es ya cumplido y cuando a
su ser perfecto (puesto que a unas más tarde y a otras más presto) llega
el punto, llega el tiempo de las misericordias divinas; porque a cada par-
tida y a cada generación, según que al sapientísimo distribuidor de
los verdaderos bienes (según la cualidad y división de las edades del
humano linaje) ordenarlo ha placido, el día y la hora de su llamamiento
está dispuesto, en el cual oigan y también reciban la gracia cristiana
que aún no recibieron, cuya noticia, con incrustable secreto y eterno
misterio su divina bondad y recta justicia, no en los siglos pasados así
como en los que estaban por venir, quiso se difundiese.

but in truth it is right to believe and to affirm that He who
formed and created the universe, who governs with gentleness
and disposes of all He has created for the use and well-being of
the end for which He made them, that end being man, with His
care and universal providence for man's perfection, not only in
that which concerns his spirit but also regarding things mortal
and temporal, He always holds, raises and inclines, and awak-

ens hearts to begin work on that which He, for his noble and supreme perfection and the total beauty of the universality of His creatures (in which in their difference and variety and constitution the order of His manifold bounties is found) all had conceived in His Divine Mind before the centuries came to be; and because humankind is not the vilest part of the Universe but rather the noblest of creatures for whom all (as we have said before) the vast structure of the world was ordained in a special and most excellent manner by Divine Providence, and, if it may be said, originially directed to one aim, to swell the numbers and perfect measure of His chosen, the copious population of that holy city and eternal dwelling place, a kingdom with all certainty made up of all peoples and of all tongues and from all places, the citizens of which will be gathered, neither before the time is due, nor many years after, but on that very day and in that very hour which, before aught was created, and with infallible counsel and with just judgment, all was disposed of; then are known and then shown and then discovered hidden nations when their time has come (some earlier and some later than others), when the time of the Divine Mercy of His perfect being has arrived; each part and each generation, by the will of the Wisest Distributor of True Goods (according to the quality and division of the ages of human descent) is exactly where it has pleased Him to place them, and the day and the hour of their calling is ordained, and at that time only will they hear and receive Christian grace, which they have not yet received; these glad tidings, with their hidden secret and eternal mystery, He in His divine goodness and right justice has willed to be made manifest at this time and not in centuries past nor in those that are to come. [*Historia general de las Indias* (General History of the Indies), I, I; written 1527–1561 but not published until 1875]

In Las Casas's providentialist interpretation, Columbus fulfilled the function of one of the chosen, one sent by God to carry out the enterprise of discovery. On reviewing the genealogy of Columbus, Las Casas notes that his very name is a sign of the supernatural responsibility granted to him: "Christopher" means "the bearer of Christ," and "Columbus" (in Spanish, *Colón*) means "populator" (or we might say "colonizer"). Thus we see how the fulfillment of objective norms reveals the way in which history is divinely ordained: "Divine Providence is wont to order that family names and given names be chosen to reveal such offices as they are to fulfill." Las Casas finds revelations not only "in many parts of the Holy Scripture" but also in chapter 4 of Aristotle's *Metaphysics*, where we read that "a name should be given to agree with the properties and offices involved" (*Historia general de las Indias*, I, II).

Columbus's journey is thus seen as one episode in the history of mankind, a history that takes place under God's everlasting protection. Future success is foreordained: God cannot allow the weakness of His creatures to stand in the way of His design, which has existed since the beginning of time. Columbus's report on his travels allows Las Casas to represent the conflict as one between the limited strength of human beings and the superior will of those who make history in the service of God's infinite power.

This providentialist interpretation of history also means that, in spite of objective differences, Las Casas can integrate American space successfully and harmoniously into the known order of European space. When he faces the need to explain the American Indians' polytheism, he has no problem in justifying it as another case of divine guidance of history:

> se ha de saber que antes que el capital enemigo de los hombres, y usurpador de la reverencia que a la verdadera deidad es debida, corrompiese los corazones humanos, en muchas partes de la tierra firme tenían conocimiento particular del verdadero Dios, teniendo creencia que había criado el mundo, y era Señor dél y lo gobernaba, y a él acudían con sus sacrificios, y culto y veneración, y con sus necesidades; y en las provincias del Perú le llamaban Viracocha, que quiere decir Criador y Hacedor, y Señor y Dios de todo. En las provincias de la Vera Paz, que es cerca de la de Guatimala, así lo han hallado y entendido los religiosos, y tienen noticia lo mismo haber sido en la Nueva España. Pero los tiempos andando, faltando gracia y doctrina, y añadiendo los hombres pecados a pecados, por justo juicio de Dios fueron aquellas gentes dejadas ir por los caminos errados que Dios les mostraba, como acaeció a toda la masa del linaje humano (poquitos sacados), como arriba en algunos capítulos se ha declarado, de donde nació el engaño de admitir la multitud de los dioses.

it must be known that before human hearts were corrupted by the chief enemy of mankind—the usurper of reverence due to the True Deity; many parts of the earth were privy to knowledge of the true God and were aware that He created the world and He was its lord and governed over it, and it was to Him they came with their sacrifices and worship and with their needs; in the provinces of Peru they called Him *Viracocha*, which means "Creator," "Maker," "Lord," and "God of all." In the province of Vera Paz, which is close by Guatimala, our priests have found this also to be true, and it is said to be the case also in New Spain. But time passed and they were lacking grace and doctrine, and men added sin upon sin; by God's just will those folk were left to wander on wrong paths, which God showed them, and this happened to the greater part of human lineage (with few exceptions) as we have said above in previous chapters; and so the mistaken belief in a multitude of gods arose. [*Apologética historia* (Apologetic History), written after 1527 but published in 1909]

Las Casas not only plays down their polytheism when he places the Indians in a historic context, he points out that Europeans were once polytheists too, and in both places it was a sign of God's will. According to his way of reasoning, there is no contradiction between the concept of the divine design of history and the presence of the devil within human society, because God allows this apparent anomaly as a means of testing mankind. The Spanish prince and writer Don Juan Manuel (1282–ca. 1349) had given a similar explanation in his *Libro de los Estados* [Book of Estates]:

la razón por qué Dios consintió que los cristianos hubiesen de los moros tanto mal, es porque hayan razón de haber con ellos guerra derechuramente, et porque los que en ella muriesen, habiendo cumplido los mandamientos de Santa Iglesia, sean mártires o sean las sus almas por el martirio quites del pecado que ficieren.

the reason why God consented that Christians suffer so much ill from the Moors is because it is right that they wage war on them, and that they die in those wars, having fulfilled the order of the Holy Church to be martyrs or that their souls by their holy deaths be rid of any sins they had committed.

The presence of evil in no way upsets the divine organization of history, since it means that God places the possibility of winning the prize of eternal salvation within the reach of all human beings. St.

Augustine says in *The City of God* that at a predetermined time demons received, with God's permission, the power to exercise their evil enmity against the City of God, inciting those whom they possessed to make sacrifices to them; not only those willing to sin are thus tempted, but also those the demons wish to ensnare, and even those who resist are subjected to hard persecutions by the forces of evil. This is by no means harmful to the Church; rather it is useful and helps expand the catalog of martyrs.

The repertoire of images that the European consciousness grafted onto the unknown space of America included, along with other constructs characteristic of the Middle Ages, an image of existence as an unending struggle to ensure being possessed by God and to avoid being possessed by the Devil. Even more, this interpretation of history made a favorable frame of reference to justify the campaign against the native inhabitants. The discovery and conquest thus became comprehensible to the European mind, since they appeared as a repetition of the holy wars, fought this time by Spaniards across the sea. The enemy was no longer the Moors, as in the epic *Poema de mío Cid* [The Poem of the Cid] (ca. 1140), or still, though less prominently, as in *Coplas a la muerte de su padre* [Verses on the Death of His Father] (1476) by Jorge Manrique (1440?–1479), but Indians. These are the new men "possessed by devils." The struggle with the native inhabitants of America becomes, in this way, a holy war to spread The Faith and is simply another episode in the eternal conflict between Good and Evil.

Although writings in defense of native populations soon appeared in America, the image of the Indian as soldier of the Devil predominates in the chronicles of the conquest; it is the image clearly presented by the Spanish conquistador and historian Gonzalo Fernández de Oviedo (1478–1557) in his *Historia general y natural de las Indias* [General and Natural History of the Indies] (1526–49):

> *Y no he hallado en esta generación cosa entre ellos más antiguamente pintada ni esculpida o de relieve entallada, ni tan principalmente acatada y reverenciada, como la figura abominable y descomulgada del demonio, de muchas y diversas maneras pintado y esculpido, o de bulto, con muchas cabezas y colas, y disformes y espantables, y caninas y feroces dentaduras, con grandes colmillos, y desmesuradas orejas, con encendidos ojos de dragón y feroz serpiente, y de muy diferenciadas suertes, y tales que la menos espantable pone mucho temor y admira-*

ción. Y es les tan sociable y común, que no solamente en una parte de la casa le tienen figurado, más aún en los bancos en que se asientan (que ellos llaman duho)*, a significar que no está solo el que se sienta, sino él y su adversario.*

I have found nothing in this race that is of more ancient date, in paintings or in carvings, nor held in higher regard, than the abominable, horrendous figure of the Devil, painted and carved in numerous different ways—many-headed, with tails, deformed, horrifying, with ferocious doglike teeth, great fangs, huge ears, flaming eyes of dragons or fierce snakes—all very different kinds and all such that the least terrifying fills one with fear and wonder. Yet they are so used to them that they do not keep them merely in one part of the house; rather, they are placed on benches (which they call *duho*) throughout, so that one never sits alone but always with one's adversary.

Every time it becomes necessary to describe the meaning of the conquest, this struggle between "right" and "wrong" surfaces in discourse about the Indies. For example, Hernán Cortés writes to Charles V that in the speech he directed to his soldiers during the march to Tenochtitlán:

yo los animaba diciéndoles que mirasen que eran vasallos de vuestra alteza y que jamás en los españoles en ninguna parte hubo falta, y que estábamos en disposición de ganar para vuestra majestad los mayores reinos y señoríos que había en el mundo, y que demás de hacer lo que a cristianos éramos obligados, en pugnar contra los enemigos de nuestra fe, y por ello en el otro mundo ganábamos la gloria y en éste conseguíamos el mayor prez y honra que hasta nuestros tiempos ninguna generación ganó.

I lifted their spirits by telling them to remember that they were vassals of Your Highness and that Spaniards never, anywhere in the world, were fainthearted; that we were in a position to win for Your Majesty the greatest kingdoms and landholdings anywhere in the world, and that besides doing that which as Christians it was our bounden duty to do, to fight against the enemies of our faith and so gain greater glory in the life hereafter—we would win great honor in this life such as no generation had ever won before. [*Second Letter*]

By interpreting the struggle against the Indians as part of the eternal conflict between good and evil, the written word erases distance and difference, and presents historic fact as repetition of a sacred ritual that extends the domain of the Christian empire. Spanish soldiers felt themselves to be on well-known ground when they could identify themselves with the generations that had fought before them in the selfsame struggle: Spaniards against Moors/Spaniards against Indians. Only appearances vary; these are still soldiers of God in the never-ending fight against the Devil's hordes. In spite of the far-flung geographical location and astonishing differences in form, the Spaniards are still fighting in a well-known mental space: the outside is made inside under the protective eye which God keeps on His armies.

Identifying themselves with the heroes of the ancient epics, the Spanish are depicted as fighting shoulder to shoulder with heavenly hosts of the cosmic home. In a letter written from Concepción to Emperor Charles V and dated October 15, 1550, Pedro de Valdivia (1500–53), the conqueror of Chile, declares he has knowledge of an extraordinary happening: three days before the battle against the Araucans, a beautiful lady dressed in white had come down among the astonished Indians and told them "Serve the Christians. Do not go against them, because they are very brave and will kill you all." Later too the Devil had appeared and "led them, telling them to gather a great multitude and he would go with them, because on our seeing so many against us we would fall dead with fear." It went exactly according to the Devil's words and the Spaniards were on the point of defeat, but in the heat of the battle Saint James the Apostle (Santiago, the patron saint of Spain) appeared and Spanish defeat was immediately turned into victory. "According to the Indians," Valdivia continued, "on the day that our forces overcame them, as our cavalry assailed them, there appeared in their midst an old, white-haired man, who told them 'Flee, flee, for these Christians will kill you all' and such was their fear that indeed they fled."

Valdivia wrote to the emperor almost at the exact time the modern picaresque novel made its first appearance, in Spain. In the Peninsula the anonymous novel *Lazarillo de Tormes* (1553), which marks the beginning of the genre, breaks totally with the idyllic vision of life that permeates renaissance literature, but Spanish America was still writing discourse as a wondrous medieval epic incorporating all the religious images of the moralizing literature of that period. The juxtaposition in one time frame of phenomena that belong to such radically different historic ages reveals the utilitarian character of early Hispanoamerican discourse. The use of supernatural and religious images reflects not only an integrating consciousness that triumphs over the unknown by enclosing it in an earlier mental schema, but written testimony of the miraculous reaffirms the positive nature of the conquest. Supernatural figures do not come down to earth and appear to men to facilitate the divine project of human salvation; rather, they collaborate in the immediate success of historical development. Their presence on the battlefield not only confirms the spatial continuity, thus making familiar the unknown; it also grants recognized spiritual authorization to concrete behavior, justifying the continuation of such behavior and assuring authorities across the sea of the future success of the enterprise.

The hackneyed use of the repertoire of images of divine will and struggle became such a common occurrence in the chronicles that Fray Bartolomé de Las Casas mentions them with ironic bitterness in his *Brevísima relación de la destrucción de las Indias* [Brief Account of the Destruction of the Indies] (dated 1552, but written much earlier). His words confirm that by the middle of the sixteenth century supernatural appearances in the tales of the discovery and conquest had become mechanical formulas for depicting events in the New World. The speed with which such visions became popular outside historic discourse and were taken over by imaginative literature set in Spanish America, serves to prove this point.

The best-known Spanish nonmedieval epic is *La Araucana* [The Araucan Epic], by Alonso de Ercilla y Zúñiga (Spain, 1533–94), published in three parts in 1569, 1578, and 1589. The story begins with an uprising of the Araucan Indians, incited by lootings by the Spanish troops under Pedro de Valdivia, and ends—after considerable structural expansion—with the final defeat of the rebels. Ercilla took part in the Araucan wars, but only from the time of his arrival with the forces of García Hurtado de Mendoza to quell the rebellion. Ercilla did not, then, take part in the events related, which occurred before his arrival, but it was a simple matter for him to inject into them topics of providentialist struggle typical of sixteenth-century chronicles. At the beginning of the tale the Araucans are viewed with all the typical characteristics of a people possessed by the Devil:

> *Gente es sin Dios ni ley, aunque respeta*
> *aquel que fue del cielo derribado,*

que como a poderoso y gran profeta
es siempre en sus cantares celebrado:
invocan su favor con falsa seta
y a todos sus negocios es llamado,
teniendo cuanto dice por seguro
del próspero suceso o mal futuro.
Y cuando quieren dar una batalla
con él lo comunican en su rito:
si no responde bien, dejan de dalla
aunque más les insista el apetito;
caso grave y negocio no se halla
do no sea convocado este maldito;
llámanle Eponamón *y comúnmente*
dan este nombre a alguno si es valiente.

They are a folk with neither God nor law,
respecting only him expelled from Heaven
as almighty god and greatest prophet,
praising him in all their songs,
invoking his favor with false sacrifices,
and calling him to be at all transactions,
his words being held as certain surety
whether success or ill tidings be foretold.
And when they wish to go to battle
they call upon him in their rites;
if he does not affirm, they change their plan,
much as it might go against their will;
no grave affair nor business can be found
where this damned fiend is not invoked,
and he is called *Eponamón*, a name
they give to any who is valiant.

According to Ercilla, the Araucans had accepted Pedro de Valdivia's rule because of their astonishment at the extraordinary presence of the horse and their terror of firearms:

Ayudó mucho el ignorante engaño
de ver en animales corregidos
hombres que por milagro y caso extraño

de la región celeste eran venidos:
y del súbito estruendo y grave daño
de los tiros de pólvora sentidos,
como a inmortales dioses los temían
que con ardientes rayos combatían.

The deception of the ignorant was much aided
by seeing men transformed into animals,
arriving miraculously from the heavens,
and by the sudden roar, then grave harm
they felt from the shots of gunpowder.
They were feared as though immortal gods
who fight with thunder and with blazing lightning.

The Spanish contributed to their own downfall. Once imperial
power was established over the Araucans, the conquerors forgot their
role as soldiers of Christ and their responsibility for spreading the
word of God. A period of cruel oppression began, which caused the
uprising, with the defeat of Valdivia:

El felice suceso, la vitoria,
la fama y posesiones que adquirían
los trujo a tal soberbia y vanagloria
que en mil leguas diez hombres no cabían,
sin pasarles jamás por la memoria
que en siete pies de tierra al fin habían
de venir a caber sus hinchazones,
su gloria vana y vanas pretensiones.
Crecían los intereses y malicia,
a costa de sudor y daño ajeno,
y la hambrienta y mísera codicia,
con libertad paciendo, iba sin freno.

The happy result—the victory, the fame,
acquired possessions—brought boastfulness,
and so swollen with pride were they
that a thousand leagues could not
contain ten men, yet never a thought
passed through their minds that
all their vainglory and pretensions

could fit into seven feet of earth.
Their covetousness and evildoing grew
at cost of others' sweat and suffering;
unchecked, greed and sensual appetites
grazed freely, roamed unreined.

For Ercilla, still a distant narrator in the poem at the time of the Araucan revolt, it is one more proof of divine providence; by straying from the divine plan of history, Spanish greed brought on God's direct intervention:

Así el ingrato pueblo castellano
en mal y estimación iba creciendo,
y siguiendo el soberbio intento vano,
tras su fortuna próspera corriendo;
pero el Padre del cielo soberano
atajó este camino, permitiendo
que aquel a quien él mismo puso el yugo,
fuese el cuchillo y áspero verdugo.

And so the ingrate Spanish settlers
grew in evil and self-importance,
pursuing their proud and vain intent,
and chasing after favorable fortune;
but our Heavenly Almighty Father
cut across their evil path, allowing
those He Himself had placed beneath the yoke
to be the blade and harsh executioner.

Although Caupolicán is the general of the Araucan army, the narrator expresses the most admiration for the warrior Lautaro, who died before Ercilla starts taking part in the story personally as an eyewitness to the events. It is Lautaro, not Caupolicán, who inflicts the greatest defeats on the Spaniards; with his victories the Araucans reach the peak of their military power. Proudly Lautaro plans to carry the invasion to Spain and demand tribute from Charles V so that he will desist in his purposes. In accord with his outstanding rank in the structural hierarchy of the story, Lautaro also bears the characteristics of a servant of Satan. Lautaro is the great Indian hero, that is to say, the great antihero to the Christians; he is the personification of a reverse cosmogony, the opposite of the person worthy of imitation in the Christian vision of history. When he threatens to drive out the Spaniards, he exclaims:

> Yo juro al infernal poder eterno
> (si la muerte en un año no me atierra)
> de echar de Chile al español gobierno.

> I swear to the eternal infernal power
> (if death fells me not before year's end)
> to drive this Spanish government from Chile.

Lautaro is fatally prevented from fulfilling his hellish threats, for shortly afterward, ambushed by Villagrán, he is shot through by an arrow and dies. This provides Ercilla with an opportunity to leave no doubt as to the eventual fate of all who serve Satan:

> Tanto rigor la aguda flecha trujo
> que al bárbaro tendió sobre la arena,
> abriendo puerta a un abundante flujo
> de negra sangre por copiosa vena:
> del rostro la color se le retrujo,
> los ojos tuerce, y con rabiosa pena
> la alma, del mortal cuerpo desatada,
> bajó furiosa a la infernal morada.

> The sharp arrow struck with such force
> it stretched the barbarian on the sand,
> opening the gates to a copious flow
> of thick black blood from an opened vein;
> from his visage all color drained;
> his eyes turned upward, and with angry sorrow
> his soul, unleashed from the mortal shell,
> descended furious to its infernal home.

Lautaro disappears from the text, starting on the fearful journey to the lower level of the cosmic home, where the King of Shadows dwells. The attitude of Lautaro's soul is the exact opposite to the peace and happiness experienced by those vassals of the Divinity who ascend to their celestial home. Lautaro's soul breaks loose from its body in a rage of fury and goes down to meet Satan.

La Araucana left behind the artistic structure and interpretation of reality of the Gothic and renaissance literary schema, yet one part of the narrative—that which covers the historic events not experienced by Ercilla firsthand in Chile—still reveals the medieval interpretation of reality which can be found in much early discourse on Spanish America. This perpetuation should be viewed as neither accidental nor surprising; on the contrary, it obeys an ideological attitude in which political, religious, social, and moral criteria function in service of a will to permanence and continuity reaching not only the first observers of American reality, but even to those who, like Ercilla himself, were beginning to feel and describe the spatial difference found in America and the erroneous nature of official behavior in the conquest of the New World.

This paradox shows precisely the extraordinary power of the Weltanschauung that the Spanish brought to America. In spite of all objective differences revealed by the Spaniard's empirical experience, the written word tries to overcome within verbal utterance, to a greater or lesser degree convincingly, any inherent differences. America belongs to the Spanish, not only by right of conquest, but as an extension of their own space—simply a new room in the good house they had left behind.

THE LANGUAGE OF EMPIRE

In the mid-sixteenth century the Spanish poet Hernando de Acuña (1520?–1585?) dedicated a sonnet to the king, *"Al Rey nuestro Señor"* ["To Our Lord the King"], announcing the imminent extension of the Spanish empire over all the known world:

Ya se acerca, señor, o ya es llegada
la edad gloriosa en que promete el cielo
una grey y un pastor sólo en el suelo,
por suerte a vuestros tiempos reservada;
ya tan alto principio en tal jornada
os muestra el fin de vuestro santo celo,
y anuncia al mundo para más consuelo
un monarca, un imperio y una espada.
Ya el orbe de la tierra siente en parte
y espera en todo vuestra monarquía

conquistada por vos en justa guerra,
que a quien ha dado Cristo su estandarte,
dará el segundo más dichoso día
en que vencido el mar, venza la tierra.

The time approaches, Lord, or has now come,
the glorious age as promised by the heavens;
it was withheld by Fortune 'til your time:
one flock, one shepherd only, on the earth.
Already dawn of such a glorious day
reveals the aim of all your holy zeal,
announcing to the world the sacred words:
one monarch, one empire, and one sword.
Now the very orb feels it is one,
awaiting and expecting your great rule,
conquered by you in most deservèd war.
He to whom his banner Christ passed on
will bring a second, happier day to hand,
when he who conquered oceans, conquers land.

Spain's messianic destiny is emphatically proclaimed in the first four
lines: now the final hour has come for fulfilling God's design, established since the beginning of time. But although it is true that the
providentialist vision still informs the text—the king of Spain is the
monarch indicated in the divine plan to carry out God's design—this
perspective is only a device and not the basis of the interpretation of
reality offered in the sonnet. What the text really announces is military
victory over Spain's enemies. Providentialism is only the means to
justify the speaker's curious way of reasoning—all the known world
longs to be ruled by Hispanic imperial might because the king is the
bearer of the banner of Christ; therefore, it is natural that he also rule
sea and land.

Acuña's sonnet shows that the subconscious image of the good
house has become a universal one. During the first half of the sixteenth century, intellectuals in Spain felt themselves to be living in a
land without borders in the center of a universal home where all
names are Spanish. With this historical outlook, a process that had
been gestating since Gothic times and which took physical reality
when Charles V assumed power in 1517 had finally come to fruition.

The new universal home has no boundaries, but it has a clearly identi-
fiable center—the figure of the emperor, or whoever represents him—
and a social code that extends its vigilance over the length and breadth
of the new space: it is the language of empire, or court language.

In the minds of the anonymous medieval bards and balladeers,
a literary work was in language open to change by all who wished to
make it. Such lay creators show none of the respect for earlier writing
that is found in the work of clerical authors. The balladeers transmit a
literary work by a vital and dynamic process, lines being composed or
altered as needs arose and listeners required. The written record of
their works came as the collective result of participation between the
initiator and his imitators, the final written form including any successive alterations that had accumulated gradually over the years.

The concept of writing as an artistic enterprise came into being
toward the end of the Middle Ages and was well established by the
time of the discovery of America. It reactivated the discourse of the
Greeks and Romans as to what exactly constitutes "correct style," and
the various low, middle, and high-flown styles of Spanish that had
been cast aside during previous centuries were reincorporated in the
written records without the result, however, of leading to rhetorical
homogeneity; quite the contrary. Starting with the Gothic writers it
had been stressed that style should not so much fit the nature of the
material represented as the social category of the person to whom the
work was being addressed and the purpose for which the discourse
was being written. In his *Libro del Conde Lucanor** [Book of Count
Lucanor], written in the first half of the fourteenth century, Prince
Juan Manuel tells us that he "maketh all those his books in Romance
language, and this that he maketh them for untutored laymen, as he
himself is not of great learning." With these words and linguistically
disguised behind the imaginary persona of an uneducated man who
writes for others such as himself, Don Juan Manuel marks the beginning of prose fiction written in the Spanish language (as opposed to
Latin). His work represents a communicative situation of a very different nature from that which existed between the bard of old and his
public: language has become a verbal instrument capable of creating
its own imaginary reality. Perhaps without fully knowing it, Don Juan

---

*In this collection one of the most popular tales, taken from Arabic sources, has the
same basic plot as Shakespeare's *The Taming of the Shrew.*

Manuel had discovered the connotative power the word acquires once it is set down on paper.

The linguistic norm of "appropriate style" forms part of Don Juan Manuel's discourse in service of a will to moralize, but once generalized it lost the ostensibly didactic use assigned to it by the late medieval writers. By the fifteenth century it had become the indispensable prerequisite of all literary composition. During the reign of Ferdinand and Isabella, the concept of "good taste" in literary language was definitely established. According to this concept, language must conform to what is appropriate for the rank of the intended listener or reader; it was, however, during the sixteenth century that this linguistic prerequisite acquired maximum socio-historic prestige and became general in all the forms of literary discourse then in fashion. In particular, it generated that specific level known as "the language of the court."

This "language of the court" was the result of an enunciative process that developed, in theory, in obedience to two basic linguistic norms: proportion and selection. The first consists of organizing the structure of the clauses in a "well-balanced manner" in order to obtain a syntax free from "jarring notes" or "irregularities in phrasing." The second requires a judicious choice of linguistic elements with the explicit purpose of avoiding vulgar speech. Good speech, says Fray Luis de León (1527–1591) in the third book of his work, *De los nombres de Cristo* [On the Names of Christ] (ca. 1585),

> *no es común, sino negocio de particular juicio, ansí en lo que se dice como en la manera como se dice; y negocio que de las palabras que todos hablan elige las que le convienen y mira el sonido dellas, y aun cuenta a veces las letras, y las pesa y las mide y las compone, para que no solamente digan con claridad lo que se pretende decir, sino también con armonía y dulzura.*

is not a commonplace, but rather a matter of particular judgment, both in what is said and how it is said; a matter of choosing, from all the words which everyone uses, just those which are appropriate, heeding the way they sound, even counting the letters and weighing them, measuring them, and putting them together so that they not only say clearly what one means to say, but do so with sweetness and harmony.

Thus, "speaking appropriately" differs from the lowly style by the interior characteristics it assumes and by the communicative and sensory effects it produces on the intended listener; it is, as Fray Luis says, a "matter of particular judgment." It became a conscious activity within the means of not just any speaker or writer, but only those particularly adapted to do so and whose aim was semantic uniformity of voice, conceptual clarity, formal harmony, phonetic sweetness, and, as Alonso de Ercilla says in *La Araucana*, though not always following his own advice, syntactic brevity:

> *Siempre la brevedad es una cosa*
> *con gran razón de todos alabada,*
> *y vemos que una plática es gustosa*
> *cuanto más breve y menos afectada;*
> *y aunque sea la prolija provechosa,*
> *nos importuna, cansa y nos enfada,*
> *que el manjar más sabroso y sazonado*
> *os deja, cuando es mucho, empalagado.*

Brevity is always a thing praised
by all and always with good reason;
we see that speeches are most pleasing
when they are short and least affected;
although prolixity is advantageous,
it tires, disturbs, and vexes us,
just as the choicest and most flavorful
sweetmeats leave us feeling cloyed
whenever they are taken in excess.

With the arrival of renaissance humanism, verbal creation forgot the spontaneity and collective merriment that characterized the creative process of the anonymous medieval minstrels, or the relaxed manner in which monks copied and glossed and commented upon manuscripts in their silent cloisters. Writing became an activity requiring "particular judgment" and was reserved for a chosen few, demanding dedication, ability, reasoning, and a wish to survive in the minds of generations to come. Written composition acquired form, meaning, and proportion by obeying norms of selection, which allowed the text to be incorporated into the accepted belief in a system of universal harmony—the high peak of success for any artistic effort made during the renaissance.

The aristocratic spirit that the "courtly writing" of the sixteenth century took on gave rise to one of the most notable traits found in certain early Hispanoamerican texts. The norms governing the language of the court were not limited in their application to texts written within Spanish possessions in Europe; rather, they crossed the Atlantic in the ships carrying the conquistadors and regulated the language of the first chroniclers and commentors on events in the Indies. It has generally been held that the first communications emanating from the New World to the kings of Spain are notably natural and spontaneous, full of "freshness" and an intimate tone born of the astonishment felt by the Spaniards on witnessing the marvels of the lands across the sea. This generalization is misleading, however, since a close reading of the texts of the period will reveal the opposite to be the case more often than not. The early chronicles form a discourse that is neither spontaneous nor natural, but the result of reflection totally incompatible with the attitudes attributed to it. Above all, the characteristic note in narratives concerning this world, which had recently been discovered and was still little known, is one of moderation. On telling of their adventures in the Indies, the conquistadors frequently adopt mentally the attitude of courtiers addressing their prince—that is, the text is wrought bearing in mind all the stylistic social stipulations mentioned above regarding the selection and balancing of words.

Thousands of miles from home, the Spaniard who reached America felt a freedom lent by distance, and, at the same time, the need for decorum as befitting his position in the new surroundings. His was a life of contradiction: at one and the same time being the dynamic conquistador and acting the suppliant role of a courtier—lord of new vassals, but a vassal of his own lord in Spain. Language tied him to his homeland and erased the distance, only to plunge him into two worlds different in time and space but joined by the written word. A large number of the first eyewitness accounts of the New World contain an astonishing juxtaposition of wild feats of imagination and well-wrought composition, with the harmony of renaissance expressions describing unbounded medieval fantasies. The language used in the descriptive texts on the New World prove the important role that the word had assumed in affirming the reality of the empire. From far-flung parts of the Indies all time and distance were erased when the conquistadors wrote back in the language of the Spanish court. Through the mystique of the word, harmoniously organized into approved discourse, American space turned into new rooms in the medieval *good home,* which had been changed into a palace covering the universe.

In adapting their discourse to comply with the rules of court language, the conquistadors affirmed their unswerving allegiance to the king of Spain. At the same time they emphasized his central position in a universe that his far-removed but ever-loyal servants were causing to expand at a dizzying rate. In 1545 Pedro de Valdivia wrote to Charles V exactly as if he were face to face with the monarch:

> *Demás desto, en lo que yo he entendido después que en la tierra entré y los indios se me alzaron, para llevar adelante la intención que tengo de perpetuarla a V.M., es en haber sido gobernador en su Real nombre para gobernar sus vasallos, y a ella con abtoridad, y capitán para los animar en la guerra, y ser el primero a los peligros, porque así convenía; padre para los favorescer en lo que pude y dolerme de sus trabajos, ayudándoselos a pasar como de hijos, y amigo en conversar con ellos; zumétrico en trazar y poblar; alarife en hacer acequias y repartir aguas; labrador y gañán en las sementeras; mayoral y rabadán en hacer criar ganados; y, en fin, poblador, criador, sustentador, conquistador y descubridor.*

And moreover, as I understood when I entered this land and found the Indians in arms against me, I must further the cause of Your Majesty and govern the vassals in Your Majesty's right royal name, and with due authority—a captain to rally them in battle, the first to venture into danger, for it should be thus; a father to favor them and bear with them in their tasks, helping as I would my children, talking with them as a friend; foremost in blazing trails and settling the land, an architect in constructing canals and apportioning the water, a worker on the land, and a peasant at sowing seed, principal shepherd and overseer of cattle, and finally founder, breeder, sustainer, conquistador, and explorer.

In general, as stressed above, early writings from the Indies were created to further simple, concrete interests and can be classified as written on request, or out of self-justification, or with propagandistic intent. The soldiers who took part in the discovery and conquest told their tales in order to be granted favors, sinecures, or simply a title—and the last was by no means the least important. They wrote to explain the reason why their conduct should be considered justified and to bear out that they too had fulfilled their duties in regard to their church, as stipulated by the state to all captains and governors. To obtain satisfaction from the power structure back in Spain, they had to convince the official in charge that spatially America had been made one with the royal lands in Europe, the new cosmic dimensions of man's home thus receiving legal recognition through the authority of the written word, employing rational argument and harmonious syntax. If linguistic requirements were properly fulfilled, it was of little concern that stubborn facts refuse to conform to the assertions of the writing. In his letter dated 1520 Hernán Cortés tells the young emperor Charles V that he may now consider himself lord of the newly discovered Aztec empire. In fact, at the time this second letter was written, Cortés and his men had just suffered a tremendous setback.

Historical reality and reality as created by the written word do not always go hand in hand in the conquistadors' discourse; the distance between their experiences and the picture painted in their writings should not, however, be considered deliberate distortion of the truth. No considered act of bad faith was undertaken in a wish to cover up the facts; rather, the fact that writing was assigned the task of publicizing rather than impartially reporting converts the writings, unknown to the authors themselves, into literary discourse. Publicity from the New World was the recognized way of assuring the king that the writer's space had successfully been added to the Spanish possessions in Europe, and it further glorified and magnified the Spanish power.

A CRAVING FOR UNIVERSAL HARMONY

The concept of worldwide Christianity, which animated Spanish military action in America, was a reflection at the political level of the cosmic sense that imbued the Spanish mentality during the sixteenth century. A literal interpretation of reality was superimposed on the archetypal image of the everlasting home. Conquistadors found themselves living in the center of a boundless space where objects became real as they were experienced, when eyes observed them. They were the focal point from which light was cast onto those objects and brought about their integration; the gaze of the conquistador conferred identity on the objects of this world.

Written discourse during the first decades of the sixteenth century is, in this sense, an outstanding expression of the confidence thinking men felt in the power of reason as an instrument to order the cosmos and their belief in the harmony with which perfect law upheld nature. Renaissance rationalism as method, and the search for harmony as aesthetic effect, are two of the most characteristic notes of renaissance literary expression.

The aesthetic code of early renaissance humanism allows no lack of balance or upheaval to appear in the natural relations of the images depicted. As the critic Margot Arce has said, every educated man in the sixteenth century was aware of the need to "dominate the urges of the wild charger;" in other words, to avoid being swept away by uncontrolled passion and a dangerous lack of rationality. The image of reality put forth by the written text must transmit confidence in universal harmony as an indestructible law upholding the home of humanity. In accord with this objective, historical existence was conceived as the object of stylized and immutable nature; anything accidental or spontaneous should be rejected as mere appearance, the aim being to capture the true abstract idealized forms of universal and imperishable nature. Vital space is dematerialized and submitted to artificial norms exempt from the socio-historic determinants that lend it the authority and justification of true reality. Human conduct, so far as literary characters are concerned, is totally removed from the social world of the period and from all the accompanying day-to-day motivations of flesh and blood human beings; it is turned into a paradigm of correct behavior subject only to the demands of universal harmony.

This imagined perfection within the cosmic home is in accord with the harmony that was considered to rule it. In fictitious works the written word stressed the threat posed by the passions and the forces of human carnality to the calm worlds conjured up by creative understanding; similarly, the presumably factual chronicles of the Indies set forth an image of a ruling process advancing smoothly toward its proposed objectives. The historical events chosen to confirm the picture were projected with special authority and adjusted to conform to previously established intellectual patterns; good fortune, ill fortune, and immediate necessity were the historical norms by which interpretation of European behavior in America should be governed. On both sides of the Atlantic the contemporaneous written word fit historical reality into the idealized patterns of a rational, harmonious, and unalterable cosmogony.

Bearing this in mind, we can say that the ideological structure of the early renaissance humanist writings is one of assured awareness. Reality, as represented in them, loses its figurative characteristics and acquires a metonymic sense of projection toward the future. The semantics of the ascendant is replaced by a will to the horizontal; writing collaborates by revealing a space that affirms a world emerging from words, its existence justified by being projected towards the system of universal harmonious values. Artistic idealization of historic reality is not simply the result of imitating Greek and Latin models but is, above all, the concrete manifestation of the renaissance sense of the eternal, expressed through images of imperishable cosmic harmony.

The dominant fictional narrative of the first half of the sixteenth century, the romance of chivalry (in English they are known as "romances," but the word *romance* in Spanish denotes the equivalent of the English verse ballad) bears the stamp of crafted composition and its characteristics reflect the then accepted image of reality. At the most immediate levels of written discourse, the images used reveal an interior rhythm totally unconnected with historical reality and everyday life. Generally the form of such tales was known since classic times, when the last exponent had been Heliodorus (fourth century A.D.), with *The Ethiopian Adventures of Theagenes and Chariclea (The Æthiopica)*. This text became widely known only following its discovery in 1534 (and especially its translation into a modern European language in 1547), but its form had already shaped medieval adventure cycles which, with the advent of printing, now bred new adventures for the avid reading public, nowhere more than in Spain. In such tales the characters are invariably noble and the plot generates its own internal motivation—it is the form where each event constitutes a semantic unit with introduction, development, and denouement; lovers are separated by forces beyond their control, then search for each other; their wanderings can be prolonged indefinitely by obstacles such as shipwrecks, kidnapping, apparent death, natural disasters, mistaken identity.* After unbelievable vicissitudes the lovers are finally reunited, and, as in a "soap opera," often bear children who continue the story with similar wanderings, trials, and adventures.

The purpose of such narratives is sheer amusement or escapism; nobody expected to read them for a sense of historical reality. The open construction means new adventures can be added ad infinitum to take the characters anywhere the writer wishes within the cosmic home. The characters themselves hail from mythic space and a time that knows no boundaries; they advance toward a horizon which melts

---

*A well-known parody of this form is Voltaire's *Candide*.

into fantasy. The tales present a reality created by a connotative power that makes no attempt to appear as anything but imaginary. The Spanish critics of the day called them "lying stories" or "pretended histories" ("history" and "story" being the same word in Spanish), and they were frequently attacked by reformers who found within them innumerable threats to the moral welfare of their readers, and useless from the point of view of teaching day-to-day morality. The complex composition of these tales in no way contradicts renaissance norms of literary representation. The extensive volume of images filling the space within the narrative world is upheld by a rigorous structural law that classifies events as furthering or delaying the de-sired denouement (the lovers being reunited, in most cases). In this way all the adventures that happen in the text respond to two forces only: the power of an unhappy fate, which systematically impedes their coming together, and a non-Christian good fortune that leads the lovers toward one another until they are finally united forever.

The early chronicles of the Indies are themselves not unlike these tales whose spirit of chivalry crossed the Atlantic in spite of moralists' qualms and royal bans, and infiltrated not only the acts of the conquis-tadors but also the ways in which they represented American reality according to the norms of structural composition of written discourse. If the renaissance novel, especially the tale of chivalry, can be de-scribed as the imaginary representation of a world imbued with aris-tocratic spirit and conduct, the first chronicles in America attempted to implant verbally the idea that in the newly discovered lands this fictional world actually existed. When depicting themselves as agents of the historic process, Spanish soldiers judged the success or failure of their undertakings to be part of the struggle between the forces of good and of ill fortune. The important fact, of course, is that in this discourse good fortune was identified as God's will, which guaranteed ahead of time the final victory against God's enemies, no matter what obstacles ill fortune might put in the conquistadors' way.

TRUTHS OF THE IMAGINATION

Of all Cortés's writings, the second letter to Charles V most clearly reveals the renaissance mind of the writer. It is dated October 30, 1520, at Segura de la Frontera—that is to say, just after the failed cam-paign to conquer Tenochtitlán, the Aztec capital. It tells of events dat-ing back to July 16, 1519, and refers to a first letter, now lost, to the

Spanish emperor. In 1522 the German printer Jacobo Cromberger, who had arrived in Seville a few years earlier, published the text of the second letter with an introductory paragraph summarizing the most important parts of Cortés's narrative. According to Cromberger, we will read "a report on the countless newly discovered lands and provinces in Yucatan in the nineteenth year of this century and subjected to the Royal Crown of His Majesty;" the rest of the paragraph is dedicated to a description of Tenochtitlán:

> En especial hace relación de una grandísima provincia muy rica, llamada Culúa, en la cual hay muy grandes ciudades y de maravillosos edificios y de grandes tratos y riquezas, entre las cuales hay una más maravillosa y rica que todas, llamada Tenustitlán, que está, por maravilloso arte, edificada sobre una grande laguna; de la cual ciudad y provincia es rey un grandísimo señor llamado Mutezuma; donde le acaecieron al capitán y a los españoles espantosas cosas de oir. Cuenta largamente el grandísimo señorío del dicho Mutezuma, y de sus ritos y ceremonias y de cómo se sirven.

In particular it describes a great and most rich province called *Culúa* in which there are most great cities and marvelous buildings, great commerce and riches, among which is one the most wondrous and rich of all, called *Tenustitlán*, which is by most wondrous art built on a lake; and of this city and province a great lord called *Mutezuma* is king; and where there happened to the Captain and the Spanish things most terrible to hear. It tells most fully of the great realm of the aforementioned *Mutezuma* and of the rites and ceremonies, and how he is served.

Cromberger's resumé becomes for future centuries the "official" way to interpret Cortés's purpose in writing the letter—namely, to give an eyewitness account of the marvels of Moctezuma's kingdom. However, without doubting that Cortés's letter does just that, it was not the main purpose of his courtly report. The opinions of the editor in Seville should not be understood as textual analysis, but rather a spontaneous expression of wonder that any reader of the time might feel on reading the report. For such a reader in the early sixteenth century, the outstanding features of the letter are those that speak of Moctezuma's royal power and give the extraordinary description of Tenochtitlán and its surrounding district. To say nowadays that the two central themes of the letter are the meeting with Moctezuma and the description of the Aztec capital only helps keep alive the confusion that originally arose from Cromberger's enthusiastic observations of 1522.

If we note the narrative order of Cortés's story, we will see that the true purpose behind the text bears no relation to Cromberger's summary. First of all, Cortés tells Charles V once again something he had stated in his first letter, written in 1519, which had gone astray: namely, that Charles may now consider himself emperor of the kingdom of Mexico "by title, and no less deserved than that of Germany, which by the Grace of God is Your Majesty's possession." It begs the emperor's indulgence regarding certain imprecise passages, "since in a certain recent *unfortunate incident* of which I will render your highness a complete account, I lost all the documents of my dealing with the natives of these lands, and many other things." In other words, the true reasons for writing the letter and the way in which it is composed are the matter of imperial expansion and the "unfortunate incident;" the letter is to explain the drawbacks the Spanish have encountered and the sad effect on the conquest—a matter closely tied to imperial expansion. Cortés builds up his account to foster growing interest, ending with the climax of the disaster of the *Noche Triste* (Night of Sorrows) and the escape of the Spanish from Tenochtitlán, during which, according to Cortés, "all the documents" dealing with Moctezuma and his subjects voluntarily swearing submission to Charles V had been lost.

Once the narrative tensions generated by the introduction have been resolved, Cortés closes his text with perfect harmony. In spite of the conquistadors' misfortune, and in spite of news concerning the Aztecs' rearming, Cortés swears he will return to Tenochtitlán and make the Aztec empire submit to Charles. His word stands on a reality created by his own discourse—the Aztec empire now belongs to Charles V even though written proof has been lost. Cortés's final suggestion that the land be named "New Spain of the Ocean Sea" closes the text on a note of success; in spite of the ill fortune that dogged the undertaking, Spain has taken possession of the Aztec empire.

Cortés's renaissance rationalism shows clearly in the outward structure of the letter; it is plotted so as to establish the leading literary motifs, develop them, and come to a conclusion, which closes the document by resolving the problems set forth in the introduction. The way in which the themes are developed within the text follows the renaissance pattern of studying the effects of good and bad fortune, the exact structure, as previously stated, characteristic of the romances popular in Spain during the first half of the sixteenth century. Cortés, with his keen political sense, has applied the laws of structural form to political and religious principles, thus legalizing Spanish overseas expansion. He has shown himself to be a loyal servant of his prince, unlike the vassals Diego Velásquez, Francisco de Garay, Pánfilo de Narváez, Moctezuma, and Cuetravacín, whose treachery has been outlined in the letter. The conquest has become a struggle by a loyal vassal to enforce his prince's messianic imperial ideals against all obstacles that ill fortune might place in his path. At this time the enterprise might appear to have failed and the forces of right seemed at low ebb, but defeat will soon pass; as in the popular romances of the time, good fortune will soon prevail.

Both the way the text is set down and reality perceived belie the concept of its "simplicity," freshness, and colloquial style. On the contrary, Cortés's letter is the finest piece of renaissance thought produced in America. Far from being spontaneous or colloquial, it is writing typical of the Spanish court—a document revealing the rationalism and naturalism of the time, organization of the discourse, political sense, and confidence in man's power to create his own protective good fortune. With the written word the future marquis del Valle has taken possession of another kingdom, although in fact it had still not been conquered. The discourse is in the reasonable, aristocratic, and measured language of the Castiglione courtier who makes history according to his will and not as dictated by adverse fortune.

Proof of its renaissance origin is not the most striking feature of the text, however. Early humanism was a mere passing current in Spain, causing the crisis that came to a head in the mid-sixteenth century; but what could not take place in Spain prevailed in the Indies: renaissance rationalism united with mythic structures inherited from the Middle Ages resulting in an intellectual synthesis that became the norm. It is this particular symbiosis which sustains Cortés's text, a view of American reality presented from a rationalist, utilitarian perspective, yet at the same time totally supported by a mythic schema taken from the romance of chivalry. This is the way human behavior in Hispanoamerica came to be defined historically.

FANTASY AND VERISIMILITUDE

The Spaniards who arrived in the New World with strong desires to-conquer materially, politically, and spiritually, also brought along a fantastic concept of reality, whose images tied them irrevocably to their medieval past. Columbus's longing to find the kingdom of the Great Khan was in no way dampened when he saw the poverty of the Caribs who crossed his path. Later, one of his companions, Juan Ponce de León (ca. 1460–1521), the discoverer of Florida, heard of a distant island where the legendary fountain of eternal youth was to be found. Another chronicler of the Indies, Pedro Mártir de Anglería (Italy, ca. 1455–1526), in *Décadas del orbe nuevo* [New World Decades] (1494–1510), assures us that there is indeed an island, called *Boyuca*, "where a notable fountain is to be found which, with their drinking of its waters, rejuvenates the agèd." Pedro Mártir never set foot in the Indies, but one of his informants, Columbus himself, would die insisting that he had reached *Cathay* [China] and *Cipango* [Japan], and that the island he called *Hispaniola* was the legendary *Ophir*, which appears in the Bible as a source of gold.

As was stated previously, the first concept of American reality manages to combine the two quite contradictory mental processes of integration and accommodation. American spatial reality is interpreted as a homely projection of everyday European space, in accordance with the medieval *good house*, yet at the same time incorporating the fantastic myths that enlivened Gothic fancy. The first writings on the Indies were motivated by a will to depict their wonder while affirming Spain's right to claim them as an extension of home. A symbiotic relationship was embedded within the written record, which, consequently, established the marvelous-and-yet-ordinary character of this world that had just entered history. From the first appearance of Spanish America in written enunciation, a dialectic dominated the written word in that the space is, at one and the same time, "the one" and "the other." This defined its essential condition from the moment it took on a historical presence in the modern world, in such a way as to misrepresent it at the same time it defined it, by describing it in terms that corresponded more to the Old World than the New.

Such representation (or misrepresentation) is found first in Columbus's *Diary*. The astonishing diversity of the aspects of the world that he saw made him feverishly coin a code of images in which the wondrous quality that makes American reality different concurrently shines through the concrete utilitarian purpose of the journey; he assures us that shortly before leaving Monte Cristi he had seen "three mermaids who rose well out of the sea but were in no way as beautiful as they are painted, and indeed, had faces more suited to men." Later, in a letter to Luis de Santángel, he re-creates in American spatial reality the myths of paradise regained, the noble savage, and the cannibal. In one of the provinces of Juana Island, which he had *not* visited, he says that "people are born with tails." Some years later he assured Ferdinand and Isabella that Eden lay up the Orinoco River, rounding out an idea that can be seen between the lines of the early diary and the letter to Luis de Santángel: "I am most certain in my spirit that the earthly paradise is where I said, and I rest my opinion on the reasons and authorities referred to above."

To say that Columbus's writings mark the beginning of Hispanoamerican "literature" is debatable. What is certain, however, is that it is on his Gothic sensitivity that an image of America was founded, and that the physiognomy of the continent and its inhabitants as described by him is with us to the present day. A feeling that the West Indies were imbued with wonder accompanied the astonished gaze of most of the conquistadors.

For this reason it is not strange that when, several decades later, Bernal Díaz del Castillo (1492–1584), a former member of Cortés's troops, writing in the second half of the sixteenth century and telling of the conquest of Mexico, states specifically that no words exist that could describe the real life view of Tenochtitlán as he first saw it; his only recourse is to cast across it the fantastic shadow of the most famous Spanish romance of chivalry:

> *Desque vimos tantas ciudades y villas pobladas en el agua, y en tierra firme otras grandes poblaciones, y aquella calzada tan derecha y por nivel como iba a México, nos quedamos admirados, y decíamos que parecía a las cosas de encantamiento que cuentan en el libro de Amadís.*

> From the moment we saw so many populated cities and towns there in the water and on the land around, and that straight, level causeway going into Mexico, we stood there amazed and said that it looked like the things of enchantment which they tell about in the book of *Amadís*.

Bernal Díaz's perspective was, to be certain, partly affected by the fact that, when he wrote his account, many years had passed since the events he was relating had taken place, but this likening of reality to a fantasy world that emerges on occasion throughout his narrative cannot be attributed entirely to the passage of time. When the Spanish conquistadors lay down the arms used in mastering the New World and take up their pens, their gaze wanders more than once from the rationalist frames of reference, which, they insist, are incapable of describing American reality. The speaker then declares his verbal impotence and takes refuge in images of wonderland, maintaining that only these can describe the space that lay before his eyes. Despite the time lapse that separates their various visions of America, Columbus, Bernal Díaz, and Alonso Ercilla all state that words cannot be found to depict American reality; all three in their loss for words take refuge in images of wonderland. Columbus's observations not only give us the first image of America but also establish the code of those "inexpressible topics" as defined by Ernst Curtius, which reinforces the idea of America as being a world to be seen with one's own eyes and not described in mere words. Ercilla for his part says some years later:

> Quien muchas tierras ve, ve muchas cosas
> que las juzga por fábula la gente;
> y tanto cuanto son maravillosas,
> el que menos las cuenta es más prudente;
> y aunque es bien que se callen las dudosas
> y no ponerme en riesgo así evidente,
> digo que la verdad hallé en el suelo,
> por más que afirmen que es subida al cielo.

> He who visits many lands sees much to prize
> that folks judge to be but tales;
> and so wondrous are the things,
> the most prudent will take measure of his words,
> though 'tis well the doubtful hold
> their peace, nor place me at such risk,
> I say I found the truth on earth,
> though they allege I've raised it to the skies.

The early descriptions of America stress first the dimension of wonder before dealing with everyday aspects; this soon led the European imagination to see America as Utopia. As soon as the first reports on the New World arrived back in Europe, America became the place where the utopian dreams of the renaissance rationalists might be made to come true, not to mention the dreams of lesser men, the lower orders and penniless second sons. Although Las Casas tries his best to show that the discovery of America is the most extraordinary proof of God's divine plan of history and that the conquistadors should therefore behave according to the most rigorous norms of Christian conduct, such invisible norms were not the ones principally projected onto the American space. The norms of a less abstract utopia predominate, which view America as a land where everything remains to be done, a space in which to create one's own patterns of behavior, a free world where the conquistador becomes a founder, in the broadest sense of the word. Moreover, the utopian possibilities were reduced almost from the very start by the Gothic mentality of the conquistadors unable to free themselves from an unconscious concept of the *good home* across the sea or from the Spanish administrative and legislative processes that converted the empire into an extension of the homeland. The American Utopia even at the moment of its birth quickly acquired the characteristics of a new land based on "home" as a model.

Written discourse collaborated in establishing such a synthesis since it upheld eyewitness viewing as the indispensable means of proving the wondrous reality of the Indies. It is true that the act of writing can create a utopia purely from fancy, but once the actual experience of "beholding" America took place, its space became framed within the possibilities of the everyday. The "realistic picture" often considered so characteristic of the artistic expression of the enterprise and fantastic concepts typical of renaissance Europe combine in the early discourse on America; sight and imagination become the two main inseparable agents in producing written testimony of the Spanish adventure in the Indies.

THE POWER OF BEHOLDING

Columbus himself was the first to insist that only by seeing can one believe the marvelous reality of the Indies, marvelous not only because it is like paradise regained, but also because spatially it extends the good house of Europe across the seas to a new world. Two descriptive processes quickly appeared to fill the demand for written accounts: the *crónica palaciega* (court chronicle), written by official writers at the Spanish court, far from the scene of action and using at secondhand other (verbal or written) accounts; and the *crónica testimonial* (testimonial account), written as an eyewitness report by a person who took part in the events of discovery and conquest. The second type soon began to contradict the first. The wondrous qualities attributed to American reality in Columbus's account, fantastic yet homely at the same time, find support in other reports, also based on empirical experience. Gonzalo Fernández de Oviedo, in Book 1 of his *Historia general y natural de las Indias*, says:

> *será a lo menos lo que yo escribiere historia verdadera y desviada de todas las fábulas que en este caso otros escritores, sin verlo, desde España a pie enjuto, han presumido escribir con elegancia y no comunes letras latinas y vulgares, por información de muchos de diferentes juicios, formando historias más allegadas al buen estilo que a la verdad de la cosa que cuentan; porque ni el ciego sabe determinar colores, ni el ausente así testificar estas materias como quien las mira.*

the least that I can do is to tell a true story, avoiding the fables that other writers, without seeing for themselves and without the efforts of taking part, have presumed to write from Spain, with elegance and uncommon Latin, history more committed to good style than to the truth of the thing they tell; because a blind man cannot see colors, nor can he who was not present bear witness to events the same as he who has seen them.

Unlike Oviedo's text, for which the attestations of empirical proof come from the fact it was written coincident with the events taking place in America, the *Historia verdadera de la conquista de la Nueva España* [True History of the Conquest of New Spain] of Bernal Díaz del Castillo (published in 1632, but written about 1580–83, when the author was in his eighties) tells of a series of events distant in the past from the time the text was written. Although Bernal Díaz's attitude is vitalist and opposed to Oviedo's humanistic perspective, both texts claim to be true inasmuch as they both present similar eyewitness accounts from direct experience of the events narrated. Bernal, a soldier with Cortés and now writing as an old man, says:

> *He estado notando cómo los muy afamados cronistas, antes que comiencen a escribir sus historias, hacen primero su prólogo y preámbulo, con razones y retórica muy subida, para dar luz y crédito a su razones, porque los curiosos lectores que las leyeren tomen melodía y sabor dellas. Y, como no soy latino, no me atrevo a hacer preámbulo ni prólogo de ello, porque para sublimar los hechos heroicos y hazañas que hicimos cuando ganamos la Nueva España y sus provincias en compañía del valeroso y esforzado capitán don Hernando Cortés, y para*

poderlo escribir tan sublimadamente como es digno, fuera menester otra
elocuencia y retórica mejor que la mía; mas lo que yo ví y me hallé en
ello peleando, como un buen testigo de vista, yo lo escribiré, con la
ayuda de Dios, muy llanamente, sin torcer a una parte ni a otra.

I have observed how famous chroniclers, before they begin their
histories, first write a prologue and a preamble, all reasoned out
and with high-flown rhetoric, to give glory and credit to their
opinions, and because accomplished readers enjoy their musi-
cal and well-wrought style. I am not a Latinist and do not dare
write preambles or prologues to make more sublime those
heroic deeds and adventures of ours when we won New Spain
and its provinces, along with the most worthy and valiant Captain Don Hernando Cortés. To write it all sublimely as is its due
were the work of another's eloquence and rhetoric better far
than mine; but I saw it and fought there, and, like a good witness, I will put it down, with God's help, very plainly and without twisting any part of it.

The successive appearance of renaissance discourse dealing with
the Indies stressed the superiority of the criteria of those who saw and
lived through the events over other accounts, and comparisons were
made in order to verify the effect of reality communicated by the
chroniclers. The affirmation of empirical truth is, then, the salient
characteristic of the testimonial account, as opposed to the non-empir-
ical truth offered by the court chronicle. Even in the case of "Gothic"
accounts, such as Las Casas's and the later histories by Bernal Díaz
and Alvar Núñez Cabeza de Vaca (ca. 1490–ca. 1559) in which the
judgment of an eyewitness participant is interspersed at times with
metaphysical argument, final confirmation of the truth of the facts
presented is always attributed to the fact that they came within the
personal experience of the author.

Many years passed between the writings of Hernán Cortés and
Bernal Díaz; their experiences, moreover, differ considerably and place
them at different ends of an ideological spectrum. Cortés wrote and
sent off his five best-known letters to the emperor between 1519 and
1526; Bernal Díaz informs us that he is telling his story when he is
"over eighty-four years of age" and has lost both "sight and hearing."
Bernal was born just after the discovery of America and his text was
written approximately sixty years after Cortés's campaign at Tenochtitlán. The time difference in the writing of the texts significantly affects

the way in which American reality is presented in each. Cortés's style is organized and earnestly serious. Bernal's, on the contrary, frequently digresses in the manner of colloquial spoken discourse. The coldness of the first text is in total contrast with the color and liveliness of the other. The greatest differences, however, are found in the narrative perspective which each writer projects within the discourse: Bernal's *True History* is the work of a writer whose outlook on life belongs to that period of history increasingly accepted as "mannerist." Cortés's letters immediately reveal the workings of a typical high renaissance intellect, naturalistic and practical, convinced of the existence of harmonious universal order, which no immediate contingencies can destroy. Interpretive multiplicity abounds in the text by Bernal Díaz, as opposed to the single-minded vision revealed in the Cortés letters. The views of reality that the *True History* puts forth are contradictory, depending on the immediate requirements of Bernal's text; the "providentialist" observations, which appear from time to time in Cortés's discourse, are simply that—observations guaranteed to uphold the official image of the conquest as a spiritual Christian endeavor, while his personal observation of facts expresses a strong belief that only the facts that fall within the realm of empirical experience can be considered real.

Cortés's intellectual perspective is, without a shadow of doubt, the one that has come to be classified as that of a personality typical of the first phase of Spanish humanism. Bearing in mind the differences between them, Cortés is to the chronicles of Spanish America what Garcilaso de la Vega (ca. 1502–36), the most famous Spanish poet of the first half of the sixteenth century, is to Spanish lyric poetry. Both were prototypical figures of the European renaissance. Garcilaso cast a cosmopolitan eye over his native Spain; Cortés viewed Mexico as a Spanish imperialist. Both were, in every way, personifications of Castiglione's courtier; Garcilaso and Cortés acted in total service to their king, to whom their submission and allegiance were complete. Garcilaso gave his life fulfilling this ideal; Cortés discovered, marveled at, then destroyed the greatest empire found by the conquistadors, all to insure his King's dominion over the New World.

CHAPTER 2

THE AWAKENING OF
MODERN AWARENESS

THE CRITICAL VISION OF SPACE

Inspired by the remains of the Roman city near Seville, a poem, *A las ruinas de Itálica* [To the Ruins of Italica], by Rodrigo Caro (1573–1647), a Spanish man of letters and early archaeologist, serves admirably to illustrate the third phase of historical awareness of the world as home. In this text the lyric voice expresses the intolerable anguish of living in the "final age" foretold by renaissance intellectuals, but one that has turned out to be very different from their expectations. Now the crumbling ruins of the monuments of the past bear witness to fleeting human vanity and to a void in the present, which contemporary man does not, or cannot, succeed in filling. The speaker is obliged to work within the elegiac frame, the *ubi sunt* motif recurring in such a way as to transcend the boundaries of simple rhetoric. His response affirms the idea of having reached a present that has no future:

> *la casa para el César fabricada,*
> *¡ay! yace de lagartos vil morada.*
> *Casas, jardines, Césares murieron,*
> *y aun las piedras que dellos se escribieron.*

> the house built for some Caesar
> is now the vile dwelling place of lizards.
> Houses, gardens, and Caesars have died,
> even the stones on which they were recorded.

The sense of disillusionment that permeates Rodrigo Caro's lines had been building in Spanish thought throughout the second half of the sixteenth century. The concept of reality proposed by the early humanists, harmonious, universal, and implicitly accepted by all, began to disappear in the works of those Spanish writers born around and after 1520.

In the New World the vision of renaissance humanism hardly surfaced with any distinction before it was drowned by the conflictive expressions revealed in a concatenation of sorrowful dialectic depicting the bounds of political power and personal insecurity, collective historical hegemony and individual vulnerability, spatial consolidation on one level and existential disintegration on the other. The archetypal "good home" had been turned into an imperial palace as a result of the historical awareness of power and the concept of national pride, which now informed the universe. There were no longer frontiers for conquistadors to push back, or mysteries, or monsters lurking silently beyond the spaces known to man. Spanish soldiers dominated Europe and America militarily; Machiavellian morals blended in a fraternal synthesis with the principles of the conquest by the Faith. The world belonged to Spain, and, as a result, the Spaniard was a citizen of the world, a cosmopolitan, the proud master of an empire, the one who had received the messianic message of the Church and was responsible for seeing it fulfilled. And because of all this, he was a person who was beginning to know the feelings of loneliness, defenselessness, and abandonment.

The first symptoms of the existential anguish that finally took the place of an awareness filled with confidence arose perhaps from the identification of the "good house" with the imperial home. Known space had expanded to such a degree that those who dwelt in it began to lose faith in the principles of harmony that supposedly reigned within it. The house had grown so large that it was a home no longer; it was uncomfortable to move through its interminable rooms, where one followed another in endless succession into spaces calling for the continual annexing of new spaces. The feeling of human beings fitting harmoniously into a universe of straight lines and perfect colors, of pregnant transparency and aristocratic bearing, was weakened now by glimpses of the inadequacy of this harmonious vision, since the true, contradictory facts of historical and everyday reality slipped through incessantly and made themselves known. The idyllic, well-planned existence that the first writers of the renaissance set forth appeared false to those who lived in the second half of the sixteenth century. Literary discourse began an unmistakable change of orientation, finally serving to tear down the curtain of myths raised by the aristocratic renaissance imagination. Contradiction became the structural law upholding the imaginary space of written discourse.

The discrediting of the feeling of confidence and the images and forms to which this had given rise is the categorical symptom of the awakening of modern awareness. Along with it, there arose a type of literature that expressed the real-life problems of the human being in society; it revealed the condition of being alone and unprepared in the universal empire where worldly goods were unfairly distributed, heroic values lost, and the human body placed in a precarious position subject to hunger and ill-treatment, where dreams were impossible in a hostile reality, and so on. These symptoms are found in the literature of Spain and in the American vice-royalties at one and the same time during the second half of the sixteenth century. In the Peninsula they represent sudden, violent change, but in the colonies they merely reaffirm an already existing awareness of a harsh reality imposed from overseas and born of having to adapt to norms governed by human greed and to the maladjustment of having to belong simultaneously to two worlds that, at bottom, were mutually hostile.

SIGNS OF DISENCHANTMENT

Although insufficient material proof remains to affirm its undoubted existence, it is known that by the beginning of the sixteenth-century poetry was already being written in America in the Spanish language. From the little that remains of sixteenth century Hispanoamerican poetry, it is evident that it was born of renaissance sensitivity but is quite different from European models, which are filled with stylized idyllic imagery, describing existence as the poets envisioned it. Francisco de Terrazas (ca. 1525–ca. 1600), who lived in Mexico, is one of the first Hispanoamerican poets whose name and works have come down to us. His nine extant sonnets, while adhering to European renaissance models in form and subject matter, show a speaker's attitude, tone of voice, and state of mind of an intensity quite different from that of European verse of the same date.

For example, the sonnet *"Dejad las hebras de oro ensortijado"* ["Put aside the threads of encircling gold"] initially appears to be a typical court stanza gallantly addressed to a lady and using stock phrases to describe the coldness of a coy mistress. The imagery belongs to the same rhetorical schema as European verse of the period: the woman's attraction is born of the cold tones of her body, the warm intensity of her glance, the color of her lips and cheeks. In abstract terms, beauty, grace, and measured conduct are the external signs of her angelic being:

> Dejad las hebras de oro ensortijado
> que el ánima me tienen enlazada,
> y volved a la nieve no pisada
> lo blanco de esas rosas matizado.
> Dejad las perlas y el coral preciado
> de que esa boca está tan adornada;
> y al cielo, de quien sois tan envidiada,
> volved los soles que le habéis robado.
> La gracia y discreción que muestra ha sido
> del gran saber del celestial maestro,
> volvédselo a la angélica natura.
> Y todo aquesto así restituído,
> veréis que lo que os queda es propio vuestro:
> ser áspera, crüel, ingrata y dura.

Put aside the threads of encircling gold
which have enmeshed my spirit;
return to the untrodden snow
that white blended with those roses.
Cast away the pearls and rich coral
by which that mouth is so adorned;
and to heaven, which envies you so much,
return the suns which you have stolen.
The grace and discretion which exemplify
great wisdom of the heavenly teacher,
give them back to angelic nature.
And, when all has been returned,
you will see that what remains is truly yours:
a being harsh, cruel, ungrateful, and hard.

Any connection and identification with European renaissance patterns is merely superficial; the state of mind of the lyric voice lacks the characteristic note of being in control of the passions, consoled by an understanding of external facts that cannot be brought under human will. On the contrary, in Terrazas's sonnet the lyric voice reflects unease at becoming aware of the radical contradiction in human nature. Hidden beneath the surface of gallant entertainment, the text painfully denounces the way in which appearances deceive. In the little we have of Terrazas's verse, this insistence on depicting reality in a way that retains very little of the harmonious renaissance worldview prevails. His sonnets transmit a feeling of anguish, conflict, and a sense of instability of the human condition in the world. Absence of happiness, awareness of fleeting time, and the senselessness of human behavior seem to personify Terrazas's view of reality.

In the following sonnet, individual existence is depicted metaphorically as a fall, absurd both as to its origin and purpose:

> Soñé que de una peña me arrojaba
> quien mi querer sujeto a sí tenía,
> y casi ya en la boca me cogía
> una fiera que abajo me esperaba.
> Yo, con temor, buscando procuraba
> de dónde con las manos me tendría,
> y el filo de una espada la una asía
> y en una yerbezuela la otra hincaba.
> La yerba a más andar la iba arrancando,
> la espada a mí la mano deshaciendo,
> yo más sus vivos filos apretando.
> ¡Oh, mísero de mí, qué mal me entiendo,
> pues huelgo de verme estar despedazando
> de miedo de acabar mi mal, muriendo!

I dreamt that o'er a cliff edge I was thrown
by one who holds me subject by my love,
almost to fall into the jaws
of a fearsome beast awaiting me below.
I, afraid, sought out with my hands
the wherewithal to grasp and save myself.
One hand found the blade-edge of a sword,
the other seized a clump of some small plant—
the harder I grasped, the looser the plant became,
my hand was slashed each time I seized the sword,
and yet I clung onto its sharpened blade.

Wretched one that I am! how little I know myself,
satisfied to be cut to pieces,
and dying from fear to end my suffering.

The poem begins as stock rhetoric on the beloved's disdain, but in the overall semantic context of the written text, the codified motif of *love that kills* loses its courtly gallant interpretation and gives way to a new, vital sensation that reveals itself as the lines of the poem progress: this is the concept of an absurd existence, the image of life as a state with no solid foundation, a feeling of reality with no roots, with no cosmic stability. There is nothing above to aspire to, and nothing below; human life is reduced to one moment of deceptive stability—it is meaningless and incomprehensible.

Another Mexican *criollo*, Juan Suárez de Peralta (ca. 1536–died near the end of the century), should also be counted among the founders of literary thought in the New World. During the second half of the sixteenth century he wrote a chronicle whose title encompasses the three narrative nuclei of the text: *Tratado del descubrimiento de Indias y su conquista, y los ritos y sacrificios, y costumbres de los indios; y de los virreyes y gobernadores que las han gobernado, especialmente en la Nueva España, y del suceso del marqués del Valle, segundo, don Martín Cortés: del rebelión que se le imputó y de las justicias y muertes que hicieron en México los jueces comisarios que para ello fueron por su majestad; y del rompimiento de los ingleses, y del principio que tuvo Francisco Draque para ser declarado enemigo* [Treatise on the discovery of the Indies and their conquest, and the rites and sacrifices and customs of the Indians; and of the viceroys and governors who have governed them, especially in New Spain, and of the happenings concerning the second marquis del Valle, Don Martín Cortés: of the rebellion imputed to him, and of the justice and deaths brought about in Mexico by the delegated judges who were appointed by his majesty; and of the dispute with the English, and of the original causes of Francis Drake being declared an enemy].

As the Mexican writer Agustín Yáñez has noted, in Suárez de Peralta's chronicle two distinct narrative tones can be found, one for relating events not directly experienced by the writer, and another for those to which he was an eyewitness. The events described in the second narrative nucleus—those dealing with the conspiracy of Martín Cortés, second marquis del Valle and son of Hernán Cortés—constitute the outstanding aspect of the work. The conspiracy occurred between 1565 and 1568, and the author stresses that he was present as an eyewitness and participant, thus guaranteeing the truth of his tale: "This is most true which I say, since I found myself in Mexico present at many events, so I know." His insistence on his objectivity is so stressed that it gives his tale a strange appearance of historical candor. For example, when he tells of the sentencing of Alonso de Avila and the last words exchanged between Avila and the priest who accompanied him to the scaffold:

> lo que el fraile dijo antes que cortasen la cabeza a Alonso de Avila, que lo oí yo, porque estaba tan cerca del tablado que tenía mi caballo la frente pegada a él, lo ví y oí todo, que era de los que fuimos con el general guardándolos y dijo las palabras atrás referidas.

what the priest said before they cut off Alonso de Avila's head I heard clearly because I was so close to the platform that my horse's forehead was pressed against it; I saw and heard everything because I was one of those with the general guarding them, and he said the words I mentioned above.

Doubtless Suárez de Peralta's emphasis on his presence at the event is meant to lend verisimilitude to the text, thanks to his objectivity inspired by observation, but his writings give the lie to such intent. Rather than an eyewitness, Suárez de Peralta's attitude is that of a personal interpreter of the facts and a person involved with those facts as he tells his tale. The picture and feel for reality that finally appear in his chronicle are the result of a *subjective* understanding of data pertaining to the world outside the text. The speaker develops the story line of the events concerning the conspiracy in such a way as to show a historical awareness not content with merely reporting on— imitating—objective norms of human conduct, but rather attempting to go beyond immediate reality to describe the hidden and tangential aspects of the events that have taken place; in other words, Suárez de Peralta's is a modern awareness in which the historian's job does not consist of depicting a harmoniously conceived rational image of reality as renaissance norms demanded, but shows rather the many contradictions hidden behind the apparent equilibrium of the objects of this world. The speaker in his text reveals a world stripped of heroic grandeur, filled with paradox and senselessness—a world where human beings are shown as dispossessed figures who have lost confidence in the stability of the vital space alloted to them.

Suárez de Peralta, whose father was a conquistador, tells of the world of the sons of the conquistadors. By the second generation of Hispanics in America—his own—the society on which his restless, critical eyes gaze, the society that rose on the ruins of the Aztec kingdom, has already changed into a fallen world where the appetites of petty shopkeepers have replaced the old will to glory and fame. Hard cash is now the prime mover of society, and human behavior is measured in terms of monetary value. In banquets for the marquis del Valle, no expense is spared: a gentleman named Hernán Gutiérrez Altamirano, "the owner of a fine estate, which must bring him in more than fifteen thousand ducats," prepared a feast for the marquis, which cost "over two thousand ducats for gifts and presents." We are informed that when the marquis appeared

> *no se trataba de otra cosa si no era de fiestas y galas, y así las había más que jamás hubo. De aquí quedaron muchos empeñados y los mercaderes hechos señores de las haciendas de todos los más caballeros, porque como se adeudaron y no podían pagar a los plazos, daban las rentas, que creo hoy día hay empeñadas haciendas de aquel tiempo. Fue con grandísimo exceso el gasto que hubo en aquella sazón.*

there was nothing but feasting and celebrating, more than there had ever been before. As a result, many were in pawn, and the merchants became the landowners and are all "gentlemen" now. All were in debt to them and could not pay their bills, so they were obliged to turn over their properties, and I do believe that many estates are still encumbered from that time. The spending was indeed excessive on that occasion.

It is not only the wish to denounce ostentatious social display that constantly drives Suárez de Peralta from objectivity in his eyewitness viewing; the abortive conspiracy, which was to have made the second marquis del Valle into King of New Spain, ended with bloody, ferocious reprisal by the forces of the king of Spain against the main figures of *criollo* aristocracy. Suárez de Peralta's narrative voice acquires a tone of radical skepticism and disillusionment at the vanity of humankind as he bemoans, with heart-rending sympathy, the ill luck of the nobles who were punished. When he describes the execution of Alonso de Avila, his "historian's" prose is imbued with sympathy for the victim in the final moment of the king's reprisal:

> *Aquel cabello que con tanto cuidado se enrizaba y hacía copete para hermosearse; en aquel público lugar donde le daba la lluvia sin reparo de*

sombrero emplumado, ni gorra aderezada con piezas de oro, como era
costumbre suya traerla, y llevaba cuando le prendieron; aquellos bigotes
que con tanta curiosidad se los retorcía y componía, ¡todo ya caído!:
que me acaeció detener el caballo, pasando por la plaza donde estaba la
horca y en ella las cabezas de estos caballeros, y ponérmelas a ver con
tantas lágrimas de mis ojos, que no sé yo en vida haber llorado tanto,
por sólo considerar lo que el mundo había mostrado en aquello que veía
presente, que no me parecía ser cosa cierta ni haber pasado, sino sueño
y muy profundo, como cuando un hombre está fuera de todo su sentido.

That hair which he would curl so carefully into a crest to show
off his handsome mien; there in the public place where the rain
beat down and with no plumed hat nor gold-buckled cap such
as he used to wear for adornment, and which he wore when
they came to take him prisoner; his whiskers, and the way he
would twirl and pat them in a way all his own, all drooping!
It happened that I reined my horse, riding across the square
where the scaffold stood, and on it I beheld the heads of those
gentlemen, and my eyes so filled with tears that never in my life
can I recall weeping so. Considering what the world revealed in
the scene I saw before me, I could not credit it, it seemed not to
have happened; rather it was something from a dream, deep
down, as when a man has lost his senses.

Through the process of writing he identifies with suffering: "It is
true," he adds later, "that I grow tender on this point with that which
memory brings back to me."

For Suárez de Peralta the narrative enunciation is not an act con-
ferring sense and direction on the world, but rather the instrument to
denounce the contradictions of authentic cosmic law hidden behind
deceptive appearances.

The story of the death penalty meted out to two of the men involved in the conspiracy—the brothers Pedro and Baltasar de Agui-
lar—cause him to reach the skeptical conclusion: "It is certainly true
of this world, and one should understand, in order to know what
happens in it, and how little certainty one can place in it." The behavior of the marquis del Valle himself is a good example of the misleading mechanisms guiding human conduct, making of it a play of
appearance and pretense. When the plotters ask the marquis to head
the rising, he will not commit himself, recommending prudence and
requesting further details about their aims. The chronicler concludes:

el marqués, realmente, él no tuvo voluntad de alzarse con la tierra, ni
por la imaginación, sino escucharles y ver en lo que se ponía el negocio,
y cuando le viera ya muy determinado y puesto en ejecución, salir él
por el rey y hacerle un gran servicio, y enviarle a decir que su padre le
había dado una vez la tierra y que él se la daba otra.

the marquis, truly, had neither the will nor the imagination to
rise with the country; rather he would listen and study the lie
of the land, but when all was underway and [the outcome] appeared certain to him, he came out for the king and did him
a great service, and sent to him to say that his father [Hernán
Cortés] had once given him [King Charles V] the land, and that
now he [Martín Cortés] was giving it to him [King Philip II]
once again.

The added notes that embellish Suárez de Peralta's empirical reporting of the Martín Cortés case lead to a definite denial of the concept of history as progress; events come into being and develop, but
how they turn out goes nowhere unless it is back to the beginning
once again. In this interpretation of history, nothing changes; after all
that happens, things are still the same except for the pain, suffering,
and deaths that have occurred. The *criollo* nobles were punished as an
example to others; the marquis del Valle did not achieve his proposed
objectives and lost his fortune due to a sentimental involvement with
a certain *criolla*, who was not acceptable in influential social circles.
This involvement allows the writer to reveal the deceptive nature of
the idea of historical progress: all forms are repeated, but with opposite meaning, as though at the end of the events the future becomes a
mirror in which human beings see themselves reversed. "The lady
was called Marina, to whom he, they said, paid court, and served just
like the Indian woman whom his father used as an interpreter to speak
with the Indians during the conquest, and who was largely responsible for its success." A woman called Marina (Malinche) helped Hernán
Cortés succeed; a woman of the same name would be the reason for
Martín Cortés's own lack of success.

Juan Suárez de Peralta claims to have "but little grammar, though
much love of reading romances and dealing with learnèd persons."
His writing clearly bears out the first assertion; but thanks perhaps
to his other interest, his text deviates from the truly historical and
veers toward the structure of the novel—it is an imaginative tale par
excellence.

Suárez de Peralta's chronicle reveals a spirit removed from the renaissance norm, and the picture of reality presented in his work definitely marks him as a writer of modern outlook with a strong sense of belonging to the New World. When he tells of the changes that have taken place in the society founded by the conquistadors and stresses, as is his wont, the absence of heroic ideals, the contradictory and misleading conduct of persons, spatial instability, and a feeling of historical circularity—he destroys the myth of the harmonious picture of life put forward by renaissance writers across the Atlantic. His narrative offers a view of history unmistakably characteristic of the first writers in the New World. It is a vision devoid of the historical optimism or confidence that human beings act rationally, which embellishes the European renaissance outlook. The elegiac tone of the speaker when referring to the conspiracy and the way in which he uses the *ubi sunt* motif do not, as they would in a Peninsular writer, express disillusionment about an uncomfortably regimented kingdom, but rather the unstable sensation of the *criollo*, who is not sure where his roots lie, since he cannot find any past with which to identify. The world of the conquistadors did not continue to his present, and the new society to which he belongs is one with which he cannot identify; America is *not* Spain. On comparing the two, we see that differences are already established; Hispanoamerica lacks a feeling of being itself and cannot manage to glimpse any sense of manifest destiny in its own future.

The generation of Suárez de Peralta—the one from between approximately 1530 and 1545—is the first to discover cosmic values encompassed by the idea of "us" and "them," "ours" and "theirs." A sense of identity and belonging is slowly being incubated but involves great difficulties due to the risks incurred by openly expressing feelings of otherness; nevertheless, rebelliousness is being born vis-à-vis the norms set in Spain. It becomes more and more common, albeit expressed surreptitiously or indirectly, as the disparity between two worlds increases. Hispanoamerica begins looking at its own "cosmic home"—the vital space that belongs to it, and to it alone. The works of some members of this generation mark the first efforts at establishing a *criollo* identity, at finding distinguishing characteristics that are truly their own, at seeing value in their immediate surroundings, and in the concept of their own difference. I refer to the first historical attempt to establish the personality of Hispanoamerica. It is, metaphorically speaking, a second discovery of the continent, one that attempts to emphasize or establish characteristics and values considered to be truly of the New World; from time to time, however, the painful feelings of dependence felt there toward the European metropolis are evident. A comparative and critical viewpoint soon emerges, and this can be seen not only in the discourse of American-born *criollo* writers but also in the perspective of writers who arrive in America from Spain and live in direct contact with the American environment.

Such is the case of Alonso de Ercilla. Shortly after taking part in the punitive expedition under Hurtado de Mendoza against the Araucans of what is now Chile, which successfully restored imperial power there, Ercilla left America toward the end of 1558 and never returned. His military service in the battle zone enabled him to gain direct experience of the Araucan wars and to bear witness to the military campaign taking place in the New World. The fruit of his experience is his poem *La Araucana*, mentioned earlier.

Literary historians have defined Ercilla's text according to the poet's own words: an epic discourse with panegyric intent in praise of Spanish imperial might, in renaissance homage to Spain as personified by Philip II. A series of elements within the text do, indeed, justify such an interpretation. In the dedication to Philip II, for example, the author presents his poem as proof of his steadfast will to serve his prince—an illustration of courtly fealty. After listing in considerable detail episodes in his life to prove his unconditional support of the Spanish monarch, Ercilla affirms that "with the desire to serve Your Majesty" retained after doing so from his earliest youth, he determined to go to Arauco to quash the Indian uprising, because

> *pareciéndome que aún no cumplía con lo que deseaba, quise también el pobre talento que Dios me dio gastarle en algo que pudiese servir a Vuestra Majestad, porque no me quedase cosa por ofrecerle. Y así, entre las mismas armas, en el poco tiempo que dieron lugar a ello, escribí este libro, el cual Vuestra Majestad reciba debajo de su amparo, que es lo que ha de valer.*

it seemed to me that I had still not yet fulfilled that required of me; I wished to spend such poor gift as God had given me in something that might serve Your Majesty, since I had no other thing to offer you. Thus, while engaged in battle itself, in the little time it took to take place, I wrote this book, which I beg you to receive, for thus will it be worthy.

In the course of the early part of the composition itself, the narrator insists once again in defining his work as a tribute to his sovereign and replaces the stock epic invocation to the Muses by a dedication to Philip II, justifying this by saying that "since it is dedicated to Your Majesty . . . something must remain unrevealed." This enigmatic reference to a hidden message that only the emperor will be able to see consists, according to Cedomil Goić, not only of showing Spain's triumph over the Araucans, but also of the image of Spain imposing itself on the whole known universe.

As a social object, *La Araucana* is presented as a renaissance work in the service of the prince; the purposes determining the narrative process have also been ascribed to the literary codes in vogue during the first half of the sixteenth century. Once again Ercilla's own words corroborate such an interpretation. In the author's prologue he indicates that the social function of his work is to win and preserve fame. He wrote and published the work in spite of the many difficulties that beset him, impelled by "the injustice that some Spaniards will suffer should their daring deeds be kept in perpetual silence." His humanistic spirit, however, not only induced him to make known the fame the Spanish deserved for defeating the proud Araucans, but also awakened in him admiration for the bravery, profound national sentiment, and sense of freedom that spurred on the conquered. He insists once again in the exposition on the double motivation behind his story: to sing the praises of the valiant warriors who managed to put Arauco under the yoke, and to bear witness to matters concerning a worthy race whose bravery should be made known to Europeans.

Renaissance hallmarks can be detected in each of the different levels of the structure of *La Araucana* but do not shape its entire literary physiognomy; on the contrary, in its essential aspects Ercilla's poem shows significant variations on the renaissance codes, especially as regards composition, generic form, and the attitude to life adopted by the writer in the middle of the discourse. These deviations from the classic renaissance poetic norms give the text a very different aspect from the one critics have traditionally assigned to it. *La Araucana* is a vivid literary expression of *mannerist* sensibility, both in its narrative composition and in conflicting depictions of reality; the earnestly affirmative discourse presents the latter in an ambiguous manner that is quite deceptive.

The two outstanding differences between *La Araucana* and traditional epic composition are the absence of an individual hero and the absence of unity of action—norms that the Aristotelian precepts insisted upon as prerequisites of an epic. Determined to compose a narrative poem on the wars of Arauco, Ercilla preferred to adopt the new structure being used by Italian poets of the time, such as Tasso and Ariosto. Instead of being conceived as a true "epic" in the traditional sense—a solemn tale of transcendental action about a superior hero— *La Araucana* adopts the structure of the Italian renaissance romance and is a narration in heroic verse about many actions carried out by many men.

Another important difference between the "literary epic" and the epic per se is the fact that the text of the first is *written*, as opposed to the *oral* nature of the latter. An epic (such as the *Poema de mío Cid* or *Beowulf*, and certainly the *Iliad* and *Odyssey*) was originally recited and much later transcribed into written discourse. An Italian renaissance "literary epic," on the other hand, was created as a written literary form and consequently intended to be read, not listened to. The classical and medieval epic is the highest poetic manifestation of the voice, a song directed to a community of silent listeners; the renaissance epic lacks the unity of focus, probably required for aural comprehension, of the earlier epic, and presages the coming into being of the modern novel (*La Araucana* was, in fact, written subsequent to the appearance in Spain of the novel *Lazarillo de Tormes*). Conceived as a written text, the renaissance epic replaced the world of traditional epic recitation, with its distancing of narrator and listeners, by a private world of discourse developed artistically through contact between the narrator and the implied reader.

This phenomenological reduction is explicit in the notion of the literary work as a *book*, as expressed by Ariosto, and also by Ercilla. In both cases, instead of describing himself in the traditional epic manner as a "singer" or "seer" whose forceful voice will fill the space separating him from his listeners, the narrator expressly states that he is *writing* the discourse, and this turns him into the familiar (to us) figure of the writer setting down events at odd, sometimes inopportune, times: "many times I wrote on leather for lack of paper, or on pieces of letters," says Ercilla himself. It is of no importance in this regard that the narrator still clings to some attitudes and practices of rhetorical recourse typical of the true epic, such as that of "singing" of the memorable deeds of a bold or exemplary hero. In spite of such vestiges, the new nontraditional literary physiognomy which the process of writing and the artistry of the written word confer on the text is the one that predominates.

However, the point of view revealed by the narrator in *La Araucana* contradicts the purposes stated at the beginning of the work. Repeatedly Ercilla stresses that the story is based on his personal experiences in Arauco. In the prologue to the reader he calls the text "a true story" and later on insists that it was written at moments seized from the heat of battle "which was most certain and true, because it took place in that same war, and with the same events and places where the episodes narrated also took place." Ercilla, then, defines his position as (simultaneously) narrator, eyewitness reporter, participant in the action, and defender of the people who took part in the campaign against the Araucans. In the exposition he stresses again that his tale is "an uncorrupted report, taken from the truth, cut to measure."

But the criterion that having been there, seen, and experienced, lends authenticity to a text, has become, in *La Araucana*, a mere rhetorical tool, a stereotypical attitude bearing no relation to the author's experiences. On the contrary, the poem reveals a world born of the narrator's poetic culture, many elements of which can be traced to the classical and renaissance epic traditions. Only a small number of the episodes related were actually experienced by Ercilla the protagonist, giving the lie to the assertions made by Ercilla the narrator of the events. His eyewitness reporting only begins, in fact, with the arrival of Hurtado de Mendoza and his troops (of which Ercilla formed a part) at La Serena in Part 1 of Canto XV. When, in Canto XII, he tells of events between Villagrán and Lautaro, which took place *before* Ercilla arrived, he goes against his initial statements:

> *Hasta aquí lo que en suma he referido*
> *yo no estuve, Señor, presente a ello,*
> *y así, de sospechoso, no he querido*
> *de parciales intérpretes sabello;*
> *de ambas las mismas partes lo he aprendido,*
> *y pongo justamente sólo aquello*
> *en que todos concuerdan y confieren,*
> *y en lo que en general menos difieren.*
> *Pues que en autoridad de lo que digo*
> *vemos que hay tanta sangre derramada,*

prosiguiendo adelante, yo me obligo
que irá la historia más autorizada:
podré ya discurrir como testigo
que fui presente a toda la jornada,
sin cegarme pasión, de la cual huyo,
no quitar a ninguno lo que es suyo.

Up to this point, of all of which I spoke
I was not there, Sire, on hand to see,
and so, out of carefulness, I have not wished
to rely on incomplete reports;
from both sides I learned about the same events,
justly putting down only occurrences
wherein all persons agree and consent,
and generally where they least differ.
Moreover to bear out what I say,
we can see that so much blood was shed,
continuing from here on, I swear that
the tale will proceed with more authority,
for I can speak as a witness,
since I was present through all events,
without being blinded by passion, from which I flee,
or robbing any of his just due.

So the first fifteen cantos of *La Araucana* are not the result of
Ercilla's experiences at all, and if all the episodes in which he did not
actually take part were to be removed, his "experiencing" could be
seen as nothing but a literary device. Ercilla's attitude is not that of an
eyewitness reporter at all, even though he says that it is. The epic
narrator of *La Araucana* shows a viewpoint that contradicts the assertions of the author in the prologue and even of the narrator himself at
the start of the story line. This contradiction reveals Ercilla's mannerist
Weltanschauung even more markedly when he tells of the episodes
that he really did experience, since these are not in the least "impartially" related, as, at the beginning of the narrative, he had so insis-
tently announced they would be. Moreover, out of the approximately
twenty months that Ercilla spent in Chile, the narrator does not mention a number of important events which did indeed take place, pre-

ferring to focus his narrative only on those in which he participated personally (or says he did). More significantly, as Marcos A. Morínigo has pointed out, he selects those incidents in which the success of the outcome was primarily due to his own participation.

The conflictive way of telling the tale and the unstable viewpoint do not mean that the text of *La Araucana* qualifies to be classified as a Byzantine romance, or "lying history," as the Spanish liked to call them; on the contrary, it undoubtedly reveals the particular historical outlook that came into being when contact was made with American reality. It is an outlook that no doubt originated from the acute existential problems which Ercilla, as well as others, experienced in fin de siècle Spain but felt even more intensely in the New World. Like the *criollos* Terrazas and Suárez de Peralta, Ercilla is an early practitioner of a subjective way of viewing reality soon to reach its peak in the work of the Inca Garcilaso de la Vega (1530–1616). The structure of the work retains the inherited classic composition, in which the elements of the narrative world are organized from a single point of view; this, however, does not imply an objective or empirical treatment of the text, but rather the existence of a relative and personal structural axis from which, in Ercilla's case, he tries fruitlessly to maintain the stipulated conditions, while observing a world whose complexity and dynamism continually oblige him to give it the lie.

This is particularly noticeable in the narrative perspective projected in the exordium to *La Araucana*. The subject originally announced—the wars of Arauco—stipulates the intention of praising the empire and bringing fame to the soldiers who expand and maintain it, but at the end of the story the narrator's skepticism and disillusionment is obvious. Praise of the empire has been converted into exposing the truth hidden beneath the lordly splendor of the conquest and the desire to honor the conquistadors is, with significant frequency, interrupted by humanistic criticism of the unjust and cruel behavior of those same Spanish soldiers. In the first part of *La Araucana* dealing with the events in which Ercilla did not take part, the image of reality presented corroborates the concepts of Spain's imperial grandeur upheld by political justice and the aristocratic Christian nature of the Spanish wars. Here the Araucan wars too are interpreted according to the "conflictive" sense of history in which reality is a battlefield where eternal combat takes place between the forces of the Devil, incarnated as the Araucan people, and the soldiers of Christ, identified as the Spanish warriors, and which still informed the political concept of the Spanish empire, so justifying its domination of America. Once Ercilla actually becomes an eyewitness to the events (as he had said at the beginning would be the case throughout), his ideological interpretation of the forces in battle alters significantly. In Part 2 of the poem the narrator reveals that the Spanish do not always act in the manner befitting soldiers of Christ, nor are the Araucans the devilish beings they were made out to be by the "informants" in Part 1. The narrator now exposes the cruelty and injustice covered over by a gentlemanly veneer. The Araucan savagery, on the other hand, is not the behavior of men who are intrinsically devilish, but the heroic attitude of a people defending the liberty that is their due as human beings.

La Araucana is, then, a mannerist text that denounces the deceitful appearance of reality and in so doing gives the lie to itself. The narrative process demythifies the official concept of a just, sacred war following the canons of the renaissance; heroic illusions vanish when confronted with the authority of the happenings experienced by Ercilla the protagonist in the battlefield, an authority to which Ercilla the narrator, in telling of them years later, does *not* give the lie. When the narrator remembers the natural beauty of the inhabitants of Chiloé in the final lines of the poem, he cannot but remark with a feeling of disillusionment:

> *Pero luego nosotros, destruyendo*
> *todo lo que tocamos de pasada,*
> *con la usada insolencia el paso abriendo*
> *les dimos lugar ancho y ancha entrada;*
> *y la antigua costumbre corrompiendo,*
> *de los nuevos insultos estragada,*
> *plantó aquí la cudicia su estandarte*
> *con más seguridad que en otra parte.*

> But then we came, destroying
> all we touched in passing,
> making our way with accustomed insolence
> given wide entry and plentiful space,
> and corrupting their ancient customs,
> destroyed by new insults.
> Cupidity planted its banner
> more firmly here than elsewhere. [Canto XXXVI]

Just as happened with the conspiracy of Martín Cortés in Suárez de Peralta's story, the denouement of *La Araucana* denies the possibility of any true temporal progress. Once the punitive war was over and the Araucan army disbanded, the narrator feels that time goes back to its beginning. According to the perspective of Ercilla the narrator, the story "bites its tail;" there is no progress, only circularity. The Araucans had rebelled against the Spanish due to the extreme greed of the first conquistadors under Pedro de Valdivia, and when Spanish dominion was reinstated, after having been temporarily lost, the original situation returned. The narrator is obliged to recognize that Spain's triumph is, above all, a final victory for cupidity and the destruction of a world which will never again be beautiful.

REMEMBRANCE OF THE GOOD THAT HAS BEEN LOST

The harmonious image of the world imposed by the official renaissance Weltanschauung broke down once writers discovered that this was contradicted by actual social and individual behavior. Subsequently, cosmic thought expressed in literary discourse was sustained by the dialectic of opposites and converted into the structural law for representing reality in artistic terms. Clearly such a dialectic already existed in early renaissance humanist thought but merely as a latent threat, the "unseen and unthought" possibility in the work of the Spanish Garcilaso. It acquired tones of sombre certitude, however, in the Peninsular literature of the second half of the sixteenth century. The new awareness gave rise, for example, to the image of life as a prison or as banishment, which imbues the poetry of the Spanish poet Fray Luis de León, along with the corresponding motifs: anxiety to return to one's origins, paradise lost, the way in which appearances deceive, and others that underline the feeling of fear and tribulation found in much of Spanish literature toward the end of the sixteenth century.

The great intellectual discovery of mannerist thought—human life seen as alienated existence—dramatically opposed both the renaissance idea of a harmonious universe and the "good house" of medieval times. Its corresponding literary images put an end to the short-lived Spanish renaissance tradition and, at the same time, introduced the vital concepts that form the intellectual perspective from which, in future, the Hispanoamerican will most commonly view the self as a marginal being outside the center of the modern world, away from the realm where important intellectual and political developments take place. The anonymous author of *Lazarillo de Tormes*, Fray Luis de León, and Alonso de Ercilla, in Spain, and the *criollos* Francisco de Terrazas, Suárez de Peralta, and the Inca Garcilaso de la Vega were all writers who, after fully assimilating the first European renaissance concept of reality, started, consciously or unconsciously, to revise critically the literary image of reality proposed by the established outlook of their times.

In their work literary representation acquires an unmistakably modern character, both as regards interpretation of the world and in the new genres that they of necessity coined in order to express the new cosmic concepts adequately. Mannerist literature tends to disdain images of idealized personages suffering aristocratic individual conflicts in no less aristocratic spaces and starts to favor an objective representation of flesh-and-blood persons who know what it is to feel lonely, hungry, and victimized. They either, like Don Quixote (1605, 1615), tirelessly pursue values that they cannot find in the everyday world, or, like Lazarillo, curb their heroism in order to establish their own economic well-being.

The material levels of literary discourse were readjusted to express the new vital sensibility. It is no coincidence that at the same time in Spain the new genres of the picaresque and cervantic novels arise, as well as the lyrics of poets such as Luis de Góngora (1561–1627) and Francisco de Quevedo (1580–1645), informed by euphuism or exhibitions of wit, and also modern drama, including the tragicomedies of Lope de Vega (1562–1635). These new norms find correspondence in the "personalized chronicle" of the Inca Garcilaso and shortly before it, in the "epic romance" of Ercilla. The new modes taken on by traditional genres destroyed or (at least in the majority of cases) altered the linguistic recourses utilized in renaissance texts. The language used now became acutely intellectual, taking full advantage of the expressive resources of antithesis, paradox, metaphor, hyperbole, allusion, and the like, and using these resources to the very limit. Similarly, there arose a new and intensely vital treatment of topics traditionally banished from the field of literary representation by the courtly sense of "measure" or "balance" (the golden mean); excess became the order of the day.

We must also not forget the important role played by *La Celestina* (1499), since this text appeared at the very threshold of modern awareness. Its generic form shows a lack of conformity with the stereotypical structures of its period. In spite of its original title (*The Tragicomedy of Calisto and Melibea*), it was *not* intended as a dramatic work; its characters' long speeches make it difficult to stage, but it is not a narrative, since the text is in the form of dialog. The term "tragicomedy" alludes to human behavior in the work rather than to the genre, since, for the majority of the characters in *La Celestina*, existence implies alienation. The story line is tragic with the comic deep in its entrails, or a comedy intrinsically tragic in itself. Written even before the renaissance had peaked in Spain, the story lay bare the false formulas to which the renaissance image of reality would conform. Heroic sentiments and social honor are shown from a perspective that ridicules them; amorous conduct is stripped of courtly dignity and revealed as an appetite whose satisfaction knows neither limit nor denial. There is no feeling of the "good house" or imperial home upholding a sense of cosmic awareness in this work—the characters move through the streets of a bourgeois Spanish town and surreptitiously use stepladders to force entry into rooms that obstinately close up their space. For these reasons, and others that do not concern us here, *La Celestina* is the great metaphor for modern alienation, and its beliefs (or lack of them) are summed up when Calisto, asked what he believes in, says "I am a Melibeist" (i.e., "I believe *only* in Melibea").

Nostalgia for a good that has been lost is the recurrent motif of the postrenaissance texts. The comforting belief in the "good house" or Universal Palace is no longer there to inspire feelings of power and pride. Instead, man feels alienated and hostile, trapped in an empty space—and this attitude leads Lazarillo de Tormes to run from one master to another, hoping to find a welcoming port at last; it impels Fray Luis to wander in anguish on the roads back to the origin of the soul; it explains the disenchantment felt by Suárez de Peralta, and the hidden deception behind the imperial commendation of Ercilla; it is the feeling of historical crisis that can be read between the lines of the *Comentarios reales de los incas* [Royal Commentaries of the Incas] (1609) by the Inca Garcilaso de la Vega. Perhaps it is coincidence that the *Comentarios reales* were published at a date halfway between the first and second parts of *Don Quixote*. While true that the closeness of the dates does not necessarily imply any ideological contact or nearness, undoubtedly the same vital historical attitudes molded both stories— the one a work of the imagination which reads like a historic chronicle, and the other a "chronicle" that comes close to being a narrative of imaginary origin—and both texts try to revive, in their present, worlds that had definitely disappeared into the past. Don Quixote would reinstate chivalric society in an antiheroic world; Garcilaso tries to do the same with the Inca kingdom of his maternal ancestors—a kingdom which, by the way, he depicts as a society ruled by the ritual norms of chivalry!

Starting from their common objectives, the affinities between the two texts could be enumerated to form a fairly long list, but here interest is only in the identical feeling of discomfort vis-à-vis the historical present, which can be found in both. With the mannerist metaphor of the "mad sage" or "wise fool," Cervantes (1547–1616) dramatically denounces the disappearance of spiritual values at a time when history is dominated by a system of bourgeois interests; he deals ironically with the literary forms that were being used in an attempt to preserve, quite artificially and at the level of pure fantasy, a lifestyle which, by his time, belonged to a time very much of the past. He exposes the society of his own time as dull and totally lacking any "noble" ideals. Garcilaso's effort is to recapture through his language the image of a vanished kingdom, and, in doing so, he puts in question the social and political structure of the *criollo* world, even though he too, in part, belongs to it. His admiration for the Incas, and the sorrow he cannot hide when he contemplates Peru's past, reveal the implicit motivation of his narrative art as being in some way an unconscious rejection of the historical times in which he lived.

The narrative program of the *Commentaries* is explicitly indicated in the proem:

> *Forzado del amor natural de la patria, me ofrecí al trabajo de escribir estos Comentarios, donde clara y distintamente se verán las cosas que en aquella república habían antes de los españoles, así en los ritos de su vana religión como en el govierno que en paz y en guerra sus Reyes tuvieron, y todo lo demás que de aquellos indios se puede decir, desde lo más ínfimo del ejercicio de los vasallos hasta lo más alto de la corona real. Escribimos solamente del Imperio de los Incas, sin entrar en otras monarquías, porque no tengo la noticia déllas que désta.*

> Forced by the natural love of the homeland, I gave myself to the work of writing these *Commentaries*, wherein can be seen clearly and distinctly the things in that republic before the coming of the Spanish: the rites of their vain religion, how the Kings had governed, in peace and in war, and all the rest about the

Indians that can be said, from the lowest in the army of vassals to the highest of the royal crown. We [sic] write only of the Empire of the Incas, without going into the other monarchies, because I do not have knowledge of any except this.

Garcilaso forces himself to write a *total* history of the Incas, beginning with their mythological origins and ending at the moment of the narrative enunciation itself; this places him not only in the position of informant about a heroic past, but also as eyewitness and protagonist during the final stages of the Inca empire; consequently, the cosmic outlook that emerges is his own, and the sense of historic dignity built up in the story must be borne in his own person. In other words, Garcilaso sees himself as the final incarnation of a prestigious kingdom, the representative descendant of an extinct race, responsible for conserving the reality of his origins through his writings.

For Garcilaso the written text is a means of re-creation and re-birth; through his writing the presence of a world that will no longer live in history will be saved by the magic of the word. As witness he attempts to historicize his indigenous past; as inheritor he views the world of the Inca creatively. He does not see his responsibility as a historian limited by historiographic norms; in his work the Inca realm is converted, rather, into an object that mainly exists according to the perspective of the writer who is trying to preserve it from oblivion.

The authoritative sources for Garcilaso's text are varied: previous chronicles, traditional tales from Cuzco with historiographic content, contemporary utopian schemes, and literary texts whose presence is implicit throughout the narration—all judiciously chosen in order not to cloud the image of the Inca kingdom and its forms of civilization. He makes use of reports from his relatives and friends, his own childhood experiences, and Inca "fables" and legends, which together help develop a true-to-life image of days gone by, but Garcilaso is far from objective: a profound sense of pain at the irreparable fallen condition of his indigenous world colors his perspective. Speaking of his Indian informants he tells us that when their tales of

> grandezas y prosperidades pasadas venían a las cosas presentes: llora-ban sus reyes muertos, enajenado su imperio y acabada su república. Estas y otras semejantes pláticas tenían los incas y Pallas en sus visi-tas; y con la memoria del bien perdido, siempre acababan su conversa-ción en lágrimas y llanto, diciendo: Trocósenos el reinar en vasallaje.

past grandeur and prosperity reached the present time, they would weep for their dead kings, for the lost empire and the vanished republic. The Incas had similar talks with Pallas when he visited them, and on remembering the good things now lost forever, they would always end with tears and lamentation, and would say "We bartered our kingdom for servitude."

It is this knowledge of historic change expressed by the old Incas that painfully colors Garcilaso's writing; the Inca kingdom that he tries to salvage from the forgetfulness of time is another good which has been lost, and he feels the same longing as that felt by Fray Luis, Ercilla, and Cervantes.

Driven from within, notwithstanding a secret conviction that his task is impossible, Garcilaso threw himself into recovering the "true" image of a lost good, just as Bernal Díaz had wanted to show the "true" story of Tenochtitlán, and Ercilla, a few years before Garcilaso, had vowed to give the "true" account of the wars of Arauco. But as with Ercilla's discourse, Garcilaso's text too reveals permanent instability and open conflict, while a solution escapes his organizing resources.

To confer universal dignity on the Incas, Garcilaso used the renaissance thesis that claimed natural equality for human beings as depositories of similar common attributes: "The Inca kings and their *amautas*, who were philosophers," Garcilaso affirms, "traced with natural light the true Lord our God." This statement varies from his expressed intention, and here too the similarity between the *criollo* Garcilaso and the Spaniard Ercilla can be seen. For the latter, the historic reality of a far from just war gave the lie to his original courtly concept; Garcilaso, who would establish the equality of cultures, for his part must face up to an unavoidable critique of his own reasoning: why was a kingdom destroyed and a civilization eliminated at the hands of beings from over the sea who were ignorant of the true spirit of those they conquered? If this kingdom and civilization differed so little from the great ones of the Old World, why should two similar cultures, enlightened by the same natural light, clash so violently, and one, graced by the same fundamental virtues as the other, be obliterated from the face of the earth by the other?

Hernán Cortés faced no such dilemma. The imperial grandeur of the Aztecs ends in the confines of his courtly writings, and nothing can justify to him its living on in the memory of generations to come; its final destiny is to be absorbed into the imperial home of Charles V, and on the former Aztec temples Christian churches rise as symbols to blot out the past.

Garcilaso, on the other hand, being of both worlds, does not wish to denigrate either the conquerors or the vanquished—an impossible situation, and his efforts to compensate carry him to the same denouement shown in Ercilla's writings. Repeatedly, the impossibility of upholding a rationalist analysis causes him to accommodate his data to fit divergent or conflictive interpretative schemata: empirical, mythical, literary, and providentialist. The key element in Garcilaso's historical reasonings can be found in Huayna Cápac's deathbed speech:

> *Muchas años ha que por revelación de Nuestro Padre el Sol tenemos que, pasados doce reyes de sus hijos, vendrá gente nueva y no conocida en estas partes, y ganará y sujetará a su imperio todos nuestros reinos y otros muchos; yo me sospecho que serán de los que sabemos que han andado por la costa de nuestro mar; será gente valerosa, que en todo os hará ventaja. También sabemos que se cumple en mí el número de los Doce Incas. Certifícoos que pocos años después que yo me haya ido de vosotros, vendrá aquella gente nueva y cumplirá lo que Nuestro Padre el Sol nos ha dicho y ganará nuestro impero y serán señores dél. Yo os mando que les obedezcáis y sirváis como a hombres que en todo os harán ventaja; que su ley será mejor que la nuestra y sus armas poderosas e invencibles más que las vuestras.*

Many years ago the revelation, which came from our Father the Sun, said that after twelve kings had descended from him there would come another people, unknown in these parts, who would defeat our empire and all our kingdoms and many others. I fear they are those men we know to have been seen on our seacoast. They will be a people who are brave and will have the advantage over you in everything. We know that with me the twelfth Inca has been reached. I swear that, a few years after I am gone from you, those people will come and fulfill the prophecy of our Father the Sun. They will conquer our kingdom and be the lords of it. I command you to obey and serve them, since they are men who will have preference. Their law is better than ours, their arms more invincible than yours.

As Bernard Flornoy has stated, these words reveal Garcilaso's prudent mestizo ear. Huayna Cápac's testimony accommodates what has taken place at the time of the enunciation in Garcilaso's text by describing events that had *not* occurred at the time they are enunciated by Huayna Cápac. For Garcilaso, to write history is to transform it; rescuing the past authorizes its alteration. When Garcilaso writes in order to fix something in human memory, he feels justified in accommodating the referent to an image arising from its own affectivity. His narrative enunciation tells a tale whose pat ending hardly meshes with the feelings of nostalgia expressed by the historian.

CHAPTER 3

THE REINTEGRATION
OF FORMS

THE RETURN TO ORIGINS

The unstable, dramatic representation of existence that materialized in works such as *La Araucana* and the *Comentarios reales* tended to disappear with the generation of writers following the Inca Garcilaso de la Vega; it can generally be said that with them the Hispanoamerican preoccupation with man's place in cosmic space receded into the background. Although their work expresses the idea of "difference" seen in the first mannerist generation, the sense of "us" versus "them"—of the *criollo* world versus that of Spain—is no longer set forth so dramatically, or at least expressed in such an unsettling way. In spite of their retaining mannerist rhetoric and forms, these literary attitudes were adopted, absorbed, and integrated into a concept of a greater cosmic unity. All the authors at the beginning of the second half of the sixteenth century, be they Spaniards settled in the vice-royalties or *criollos* born in the New World, received their intellectual formation during the years when norms of social, artistic, and moral behavior were imposed as a result of the edicts of the Council of Trent (1545–63), called by the Roman Catholic Church to discuss means of countering the Reformation. From the ideological point of view at least, their literary work shows a decided wish to return to and reintegrate with their origins, an attitude that distances them considerably from the conflictive, unstable, creative intellectual behavior of the first mannerists. The works of Bernardo de Balbuena (Spain, ca. 1561–New Spain [Mexico], 1627), Juan Rodríguez Freile (New Granada [Colombia], 1566–ca. 1640), Pedro de Oña (Chile, 1570–ca. 1643), Diego de Hojeda (Spain, 1571–Peru, 1615), and Francisco Bramón (Mexico, died after

1654), among others, move in two directions—developing stylistically while backtracking intellectually; their work shows a more advanced literary technique, or, if this is not the case, as with Rodríguez Freile, a better defined creative consciousness than their immediate predecessors. At the same time, the way they interpret reality lacks the dynamic, vital spirit found in the works of the authors born just before the midpoint of the sixteenth century.

In the colonies the need to comply with the norms of moral conduct set down by the Counter-Reformation assumed political, as well as moral, imperatives, and to question the Church was political treason as well as religious heresy and punishable as such; to this can be attributed the notable change that these authors reveal in their way of understanding the concept and function of literature. For them, a literary work was, above all, an expression of heroic religious ideals, an apologetic or laudatory discourse of ethical purpose, or, if none of these, testimony to the holiness of human history. In one way or another, literature went back to being the edifying discourse that the scholastics had assigned to it before the humanist and mannerist hiatus.

A characteristic sign of the new way in which literature, and consequently creative activity, worked, is the appearance of a profuse amount of sacred literature in the seventeenth century panorama. Along with allegorical or apostolic dramas that filled the newly established stages of Hispanoamerica, we find an abundance of new hagiographic narrative telling of the lives of saints, prodigies, martyrs; of colonial ecclesiastical activities; and religious epic poems: *La cristiada* [The Christiad] (1611) by Fray Diego de Hojeda, *Poema a la canonización de los veintitrés mártires del Japón* [Poem on the Canonization of the Twenty-Three Martyrs in Japan] (1630) by Fray Juan de Ayllón (Peru, 1604–?), *San Ignacio de Cantabria* (1639) by Pedro de Oña, *Poema heroico de San Ignacio de Loyola* [Heroic Poem on St. Ignatius Loyola] (1666) by Hernando Domínguez Camargo (New Granada [Colombia], 1606–59). Except for isolated cases, these works offer as their plot the lives of exemplary figures from places far removed geographically from the place where they were written, and in this sense, they signify a retrogression parallel to the intellectual paralysis that Spain suffered at the same time.

This intellectual stagnation is especially obvious in the return to earlier forms and in the reintegrative semantics that the texts reveal.

La cristiada, for example, throws out all the mannerist innovations introduced in *La Araucana* and returns to earlier norms of action and characterization in order to focus the reader's interest on the religious message the speaker is attempting to transmit:

> *Canto al Hijo de Dios, humano, y muerto*
> *con dolores y afrenta por el hombre.*
> *Musa divina, en su costado abierto*
> *baña mi lengua y muévela en su nombre,*
> *porque suene mi voz con tal concierto,*
> *que, los oídos halagando, asombre*
> *al rudo y sabio, y el cristiano gusto*
> *halle provecho en un deleite justo.*
> *Dime también los pasos que obediente*
> *desde el Huerto al Calvario Cristo anduvo,*
> *preso y juzgado de la fiera gente*
> *que, viendo a Dios morir, sin miedo estuvo;*
> *y el edificio de almas eminente*
> *que, cansado y herido, en peso tuvo;*
> *de ilustres hijos el linaje santo,*
> *del cielo el gozo y del infierno el llanto.*

I sing to the Son of God, human, yet killed
by the sorrows and insults of man.
Divine Muse, in the open wound of His side
bathe my tongue and move it in His name
so my voice resound with such harmony
that, flattering the ears, it will surprise
the rude listener, and the wise,
and Christian taste find profit in just delight.
Tell me, too, of the steps which obediently
from the Garden to Calvary Christ took
while prisoner and judged by cruel folk,
who, seeing God die, were without fear;
of that eminent edifice of souls
which he bore though tired and wounded,
of the holy lineage of famous sons,
of the joy of Heaven and wails from Hell. (Book 1)

This return to earlier literary structures was the immediate result of fear of the historical changes that came into effect in the second half of the sixteenth century, a fear made manifest by attitudes of artistic regression and the shunning of non-conformity. Fray Diego de Hojeda, in his dedication to the marquis de Montesclaros, Viceroy of Peru, declares with spontaneous and enlightening sincerity:

> La vida de Cristo Nuestro Señor escrita en verso ofrezco a Vuestra Excelencia, por el sujeto merecedora de altísima veneración, y por el estilo antiguamente estimada, y ya (no sé por qué) no tanto.

The life of our Lord Jesus Christ, written in verse, is offered to Your Excellency because of the subject, which is worthy of the highest veneration, and in a style which used to be highly esteemed also, but which nowadays (I do not know why) is not esteemed so much.

The result of this denial of historical process, or the incapacity to understand it, was that Hispanoamerica never fully developed a concept of literature as the expression of the ideals of renaissance humanism, while the mannerist concept expressing the existential and social conflict of the individual could not openly proceed further. Literature became an instrument for ethical and religious edification in service of the ideals and norms of conduct imposed by post-Tridentine Catholicism.

In spite of the utilitarian function resumed by literature in Hispanoamerica, it did not adopt anew the popular language that had been used to communicate "revealed truth" to medieval listeners. Fray Diego de Hojeda, in common with most Hispanoamerican baroque writers, could not bring himself to reject the formal renovations that the Spanish mannerists had imposed. His high-flown classical references, his preciosity of style, and the syntactic characteristics of his discourse reveal the writer's urbanity and separate this religious epic from popular medieval hagiography. The effectiveness of the ethical message of The Christiad is thus limited to a cultural minority capable of deciphering the edifying signs from the linguistic forms the narrator manipulates.

Profane literature also lost the new ideas it had acquired along with mannerist sensitivity. In Arauco domado [Arauco Subdued] (1596) Pedro de Oña has rewritten La Araucana to correct the interpretation of reality that Ercilla had set forth, and, in so doing, destroyed the valuable new qualities that Ercilla had brought to the genre, as well as the modern vision of the world he had offered. Not only that; in the final years of the sixteenth century the aristocratic interpretation of reality—which renaissance authors had attempted to impose with limited success at the beginning of the century—was imposed once again. The conflictive mannerist vision of existence, as well as the humanistic criticism of history, has disappeared from *Arauco domado*. Precisely because Oña was a *criollo* of the last half of the sixteenth century, he could not see what Ercilla is denouncing in his work—namely, the arbitrariness with which the Spanish soldiers behaved once they were far from their home space and their king, and how this denoted the failure of the humanist and Christian principles that were the official reasons given for undertaking the conquest in the first place.

One of the writers who best represents the intellectual regression patent in Hispanoamerican letters from the beginning of the seventeenth century is Bernardo de Balbuena. His major works all reveal the conservative's desire to turn back the clock, to return to one's origins, to be once again in the "good home" left behind by his immediate literary predecessors. Although his texts fit comfortably into the first half of the seventeenth century, they do not all adopt the new literary structures of Spanish letters, nor much less reveal the conflictive and polemic vision of reality typical of those structures. In 1592 he began to write a long epic poem *El Bernardo o Victoria de Roncesvalles* [The Story of Bernardo del Carpio, or Victory at Roncesvalles] on the eighth-century battle, which was not published until 1624. The subject matter clearly reveals the wish to go back in time and a lack of interest in the things of the present; the author would rather submerge himself in a glorious Spanish past that appeared to him to be more valuable than the Hispanoamerican present in which he was living. In 1602 he had written his only work connected in any way with his own historic period: *Grandeza mexicana* [Mexican Grandeur] (pub. 1604), which, in spite of the title, is fundamentally nothing more than the total confirmation of the wish to return to roots, which informs his work. In 1608 he published (in Spain) *Siglo de oro en las selvas de Erífile* [The Golden Age in the Forest of Eriphyle], a pastoral novel, when the form had already virtually fallen into disuse.

It is for *Grandeza mexicana* that Balbuena is best remembered today. The structure of the work is quite simple, consisting of nine "chapters" in verse, each of which is an expansion of the images summarized in the eight-line stanza called the *Argument* at the beginning of the work:

De la famosa México el asiento,
origen y grandeza de edificios,
caballos, calles, trato, cumplimiento,
letras, virtudes, variedad de oficios,
regalos, ocasiones de contento,
primavera inmortal y sus indicios,
gobierno ilustre, religión y Estado,
todo en este discurso está cifrado.

Of the famous Mexico the seat,
origin and grandeur of buildings,
horses, streets, commerce, civility,
letters, virtues, variety of occupations,
gifts, pastimes and amusements,
eternal spring and its signs, illustrious
government, religion, Commonwealth,
all in this discourse are summarized.

Each chapter develops similarly: the speaker compares the city to homologous cultural elements found elsewhere, always affirming the superiority of Mexico City over everywhere else. From a rhetorical point of view, each chapter can be said to be an extensive linguistic development of the then fashionable hyperbolic device of *sobrepujamiento* (baroque excess), found in precious or euphuistic verse of the mannerist and baroque periods, in which the speaker grandiloquently inflates his laudatory material to exasperating limits.

This sustained attitude of eulogy has an immediate purpose: to demonstrate that Mexico City is the mythic point toward which the history of humanity flows and where it reaches its epitome; it is "the center of perfection, the hinge of the world," a privileged space in which everything culminates and sense and order are perfected. The piling up of images, the interminable enumerations, hyperbole, rhetorical questions, and the like—all placed at the service of the tireless laudatory expressions—the rhythmic cadence within each chapter and the emphatic conclusions are some of the techniques used by the speaker to construct the image of Mexico City as focal point and final outcome of the progress of history. The city is metamorphosed in a visionary manner into the hub of divine and human creation, into the sacred center of the universe where any conflicts with the surrounding space are definitively and imperishably reconciled. From the lake on which Mexico City is built flows "all that human genius forges, art achieves, and desire expresses;" the grandeur of other important buildings cited by history is merely "a shadow" of that of the Mexican edifices, "and if there is more than this, even that you [Mexico City] will have." All the virtues that heaven has put in the world "will be found here by whoever tries to find them, and more than this, if more is desired;" so many gifts and so many occasions for satisfaction that "covetousness and desire can be enhanced and still possess the thing desired, here one can be content, and here I see it, and here they have their share in its sphere;" the unimaginable qualities of the spring: "here with a thousand beauties and benefits all given by the sovereign hand."

Nevertheless, the laudatory character of Balbuena's discourse is somewhat misleading. The work was written at the request of Doña Isabel de Tobar y Guzmán (the sister of the viceroy) that Balbuena describe Mexico City in writing. The praise that resulted from this petition is justified by the author himself as the consequence of the "great veneration and respect in which I have always held such things, since they seem to be worthy of this recognition, and this place, from among so many, has to this very day held my esteem," but in the denouement of the final chapter of the poem we see that Balbuena's true but hidden purpose contradicts what he said at the beginning. Only when readers reach the final lines can they understand that the dazzling image of Mexico City has been masking the true referent of the story, which is not Mexico City at all, but the Spain of Philip III, and that Balbuena's real purpose has been to convert Mexico City into the luminous cosmic symbol of the grandeur of imperial Spain.

The surprising alteration of the sense of the poem justifies the change of intended reader, which the final lines produce. The basic linguistic attitude adopted by the speaker throughout the text is one of apostrophe, but the specified reader, Doña Isabel de Tobar y Guzmán, is replaced in the epilogue by the "sweet homeland," the Spain of Philip III, where the narrator expresses his ardent desire to return, either alive or after death. This "sweet homeland" regenerates, then, in the awareness of the speaker, the medieval notion of the "good house," the original protective space that had been abandoned and to which he now most fervently wishes to return:

¡Oh, España altiva y fiel, siglos dorados
los que a tu monarquía han dado priesa,

y a tu triunfo mil reyes destocados!
Traes al Albis rendido, a Francia presa,
humilde al Poo, pacífico al Toscano,
Túnez en freno, Africa en empresa.
Aquí te huye un príncipe otomano;
allí rinde su espada a la vislumbre
de la desnuda espada de tu mano.
Ya das ley a Milán, ya a Flandes lumbre;
ya el Imperio defiendes y eternizas,
o a la Iglesia sustentas en su cumbre;
el mundo que gobiernas y autorizas
te alabe, patria dulce, y a tus playas
mi humilde cuerpo vuelva, o sus cenizas.
Y pues ya el cetro general te ensayas,
con que dichosamente el cielo ordena
que en triunfal carro de oro por él vayas,
entre el menudo aljófar que a su arena
y a tu gusto entresaca el indio feo,
y por tributos dél tus flotas llena,
de mi pobre caudal el corto empleo
recibe en este amago, do presente
conozcas tu grandeza, o mi deseo
de celebrarla al mundo eternamente.

Oh, Spain, proud and faithful, golden centuries
are those which have spurred thy monarchy,
and to thy triumph a thousand kings bared their heads!
Thou hast subdued Albis, seized France,
humbled the Po, pacified the Tuscans,
reined in Tunis, campaigned in Africa.
Here an Ottoman prince flees before thee,
there he yields his sword at the glimmer
of the unsheathed blade in thy hand.
Thou givest law to Milan, to Flanders light,
and dost the Empire defend and perpetuate,
or support the Church at its peak;
let the world which thou dost govern

praise thee, sweet homeland. And to thy shores
return my humble body, or its ashes.
Now dost thou grasp the general scepter
with which Heaven doth joyously ordain
that in triumphant golden coach thou shouldst go forth,
and for thy pleasure the ugly Indian doth select
from among the pearls of this his land
to fill thy fleet with his tribute;
accept this short work from my poor source,
this trifle wherein presently
thou shalt see thy greatness, or my desire
to sing it to the world forevermore.

The conclusion of *Grandeza mexicana* provides the key for an understanding of the development of the text. The speaker has given a dazzling description of Mexico City, but has always had in mind the image of the distant "good house" in Spain, proud and faithful "sweet homeland," conquerer and ruling power of the known world. Ironically, at the end, praise of the city is combined with praise for its position as a privileged payer of tribute to the European metropolis; the lustrous catalog of Mexican riches is there to justify that the "ugly Indian" fill the holds of the Spanish fleet with the riches of the American world.

Although the perspective of the speaker in *Grandeza mexicana* seems marked by ideological references typical of the Hispanoamerican baroque, the composition of the poem involves a mannerist form similar to that of *La Araucana*; in both cases the speaker concentrates his attention on one element of the text's imaginary space, implicitly to move his interest later to a contrary, or hidden, element: the narrator of Ercilla's text systematically inflates the Araucans to enhance Spanish prowess indirectly; the speaker in Balbuena's poem, on the other hand, concentrates his praise on Mexico to show the value of the city at the end as a symbolic projection of the splendor of Spain. There is an obvious difference, however, which reveals the ideological distance between the two works. Ercilla cannot uphold the narrator's perspective, because his own purpose in writing gives it the lie; Balbuena, on the other hand, maintains his purpose with impunity for the full length of the text, since he is not a humanist critic such as Ercilla, thus his imperial regard is undamaged. For Balbuena no shadows cloud over the results of the conquest. Having unreservedly praised Mexico City, he demands of the world that Spain "govern and authenticate" it and that it pay the homage the "sweet homeland" deserves.

THE REBIRTH OF THE OLD-FASHIONED NOVEL

Balbuena's will to reintegration recalls the cultural context in which the early Hispanoamerican novel was born. As is well known, from its beginnings in the sixteenth century this genre was enthusiastically received by the public, but awakened adverse criticism from moralists who viewed the growing popularity of these "lying stories" with dismay and even suppressed them completely with unequivocal moral violence. Referring to the books of chivalry, the Spanish humanist, Juan Luis Vives (1492–1540), says that they were "written by lazy men with nothing better to do, unlettered, full of vice and filth;" their popularity was attributed to their being wildly imaginative with a capacity to arouse vices in the readers. Vives wonders "How can a thing either of doctrine or virtue be provided by those who never saw it with their own eyes?" (*Instrucción de la mujer cristiana* [Instruction of the Christian Woman], 1524).

Starting with Vives, warnings of the moral dangers inherent in these profane tales, especially the ones of chivalry, are found throughout the sixteenth century. They form part of the ideological background that gave rise, in part, to the royal decrees, dating from 1531, which prohibited the export of such books to the Indies; only in part, however, because, as Francisco Rodríguez Marín has observed, the cautious attitude of the authorities toward escapist narratives were due to different reasons in Spain from those in the Indies. In the Peninsula the warnings of the moralists were principally directed at the young, and the emphasis was on the moral danger that reading such books could cause inexperienced readers. In the decrees of 1531 and 1543 on the Indies, the authorities did not have in mind young Spaniards in America, but were worried about Indian converts whose new and still precarious Catholic faith might be endangered by reading these texts, and, without stating it openly, what the authorities were really afraid of was the possible political consequences for the cohesion of the Empire if the spiritual union were weakened.

In spite of the official prohibitions, chivalric novels still kept arriving in the New World, either in the memory of the conquistadors, or in shipments that regularly left Spain for the Indies. However, the first Hispanoamerican writers, either *criollo* or Spanish-born, preferred to dedicate their efforts to writing other genres: epic narrative, lyric poetry, missionary drama, and, above all, a profusion of eyewitness informative accounts that filled the intellectual life of Hispanoamerica in its early years, but are not (or were not), properly speaking, usually classified as "literature." This lack of interest in the novelistic form, which would have reproduced in the American medium the imaginative characteristics of the European novel and presented American reality in fictional space, lasted through the three centuries that constitute the Spanish colonial period in the New World. All that stands out from this barren novelistic panorama are a very few isolated attempts at narrative in which the form more or less approaches a novelistic structure; for example: *Siglo de oro en las selvas de Erífile* by Bernardo de Balbuena, *Los sirgueros de la Virgen sin original pecado* [The Songbirds of the Virgin without Original Sin] (1620) by Francisco Bramón, *El pastor de nochebuena* [The Christmas Shepherd] (1644) by Juan de Palafox (Spain, 1600–Mexico, 1659), and *Infortunios de Alonso Ramírez* [Misfortunes of Alonso Ramírez] (1690) by Carlos de Sigüenza y Góngora (Mexico, 1645–1700).

It is interesting that of these four tales, the three that dominated the seventeenth-century Hispanoamerican panorama either belong to the pastoral tradition, as in the case of Balbuena and Bramón, or use a shepherd to trigger the events, as in Palafox's allegory. Only in Sigüenza's work at the end of the 1600s are there slight tinges of the picaresque, which had developed in Spain in the middle of the previous century. It might be suspected that the total absence of the novel of chivalry or Byzantine romance, which had been the most prestigious of the old forms, as well as the absence of the picaresque, which had replaced them in popularity, is due to the fact that they express types of historical awareness that did not exist within the newly developing social structures of sixteenth-, seventeenth-, and eighteenth-century Hispanoamerica. From an early date the *criollo* society of the New World was bourgeois in that its ideals were alien to the values that determined the function and upheld the structure of the chivalric or Byzantine novel. The picaresque, on the other hand, developed in Spain as a means of criticizing and denouncing the new bourgeois society already established there by the sixteenth century, while this type of society did not arise in Hispanoamerica until well into the seventeenth.

The early Hispanoamerican novels, then, chose to ignore the historical or critical development of the Peninsular novel and chose to follow the pastoral pattern at a time when it was already in decline in Spain after a reign there of over fifty years. Pastoral imagery did not maintain its original literary function in the New World, but was directed to the ethical improvement of the intended reader and the formation of spiritual values deemed necessary to guide the newly created Hispanoamerican society toward its metaphysical destiny. This ideological orientation can be seen very clearly in Francisco Bramón's work, *Los sirgueros de la Virgen sin original pecado*, the first real Spanish-American novel, since Balbuena's *Siglo de oro*, though earlier, was, after all, published in Spain. It is a pastoral novel that totally ignores the innovations of the picaresque, utilizing the baroque *pastoril a lo divino* variant—that is, rewriting a "profane" story "in the divine manner," which corresponds to the period of historical decadence of the genre in Spain.

At its most immediate level the story of *Los sirgueros de la Virgen* clearly adopts the techniques of the old-fashioned pastoral novel: an impersonal and omniscient narrator presents a pastoral world preparing for a celebration in honor of a lady of superior quality. All confess that they adore her. The text begins with a traditional pastoral motif: in the middle of an archetypical atmosphere, the shepherdess Marcilda is described:

> *pimpollo de hermosura, pastora de edad perfecta; en sus razones dulce, sabia y elocuente; en su grave y recogida vista, apacible; en sus palabras, amorosa, y en ellas muy medida; grave en su presencia; y en cualquier inclinación y arte, tan avisada y sagaz, que la celebran por oráculo en aquel ameno y rico prado.*

> a beautiful rosebud, a shepherdess of the perfect age; sweetly reasonable, knowledgeable and eloquent; in her grave and retiring appearance meek and gentle; in her speech loving and measured; grave in presence; prudent and wise in all her inclinations and arts; so that they held her to be an oracle in that pleasant and rich meadow.

She dedicates her time to "reflecting under a leafy plantain." The concept of Marcilda never develops as might be imagined, however; the characteristic pastoral motif of pain or sorrow due to the absence of the beloved shepherd and the discourse that follows do not appear in the expected forms. "With tender sighs born from inside her breast," Marcilda dedicates herself to "considering the great loss that the orig-

inal sin of Adam, our first father" incurred. The story is then immediately programed as a form of recovering the transcendent sense of
human existence. A little further on in the text, this sense is reinforced
when the reader discovers that the lady in whose honor the celebration being held is, in fact, the Virgin Mary, and that the admiration of
all the shepherds is a holy love. This is one of the earliest literary
works to put forth the idea of the Immaculate Conception, though
it was not promulgated as Church dogma until two hundred fifty
years later.

Adjusting a profane story to turn it into exemplary form gives
rise to a series of equivocal situations, conventionally solved conflicts,
and communication through an intermediary. All this, combined with
the ambiguous direction of the dialog, repeated interaction between
levels that are imaginary or extraliterary to the reality of the text, and
the figure of the author reflected in the character Anfriso, make this
another text of the typical mannerist outlook that dominated early
Hispanoamerican literature. But the mannerist interpretation of reality
revealed in Bramón's novel differs completely from that shown by the
generation of Ercilla, the Inca Garcilaso, Suárez de Peralta, and Terrazas. The feeling of conflict that these writers find in human behavior
was generated basically by their lack of confidence in the harmonious
and regulated concept of the universe put forth by the first humanists
in ideological support of imperial expansion. The structural ambiva-
lence of *Los sirgueros de la Virgen* is, on the contrary, the consequence
of an attempt to convert the profane into a sacred form—that is to say,
to reestablish the depiction of the transcendent as found in medieval
representations of reality. Any maladjustment is provoked by the attempt to set back the clock, by the desire to find again the protecting
structures of a now alien past. The disagreement between the artificial
image of reality and the ethically edifying intent in Bramón's novel is
a significant illustration of the way in which critically alert Hispanoamerican mannerist thought was now being redirected to accommodate the regulated medievalist perspective of the baroque.

THE HIDDEN TRUTHS OF REALITY

El carnero (1636), by Juan Rodríguez Freile, has a contemporary air
that surprises the reader from its very beginning. The easy freedom of
the speaker in developing his story is the sign of an intuitive awareness that we think of as modern, and his fresh spontaneity goes much

further than it would in a true historical chronicle, the form the author himself says is the model of his story.

With acute perspicacity, the first readers of *El carnero* discovered the contradiction between the original title of the work, *Conquista y descubrimiento del Nuevo Reino de Granada* [The Conquest and Discovery of the New Kingdom of Granada], and the structure and levels of meaning in the text. The original title did not for one moment pull the wool over the eyes of the first readers, who immediately nicknamed it *El carnero* [The Ram]. (The precise significance of this alternate title has never been established, with certainty, even today.) Contrary to the words of the author, readers realized that the story was pointing toward the representation of spheres of reality alien to those covered by traditional chronicles. In any case, the double name, one given by the author and one by the public, reveals the antithesis between the true literary personality of Rodríguez Freile's work and the form of testimonial chronicle attributed to it by its author. In fact, *El carnero* turns out to be the reverse of what it says it is.

El carnero cannot truly be described as a "literary" work; the language used does not fulfill the representative or mimetic function sufficiently to classify the story as a "work of art," but neither is it a simple pedestrian account. It tells the history of New Granada from the pre-Hispanic period to the time it was being written, but the picture it gives is one of the writer struggling to complete the parts of the text involved with the historical account in order to submerge himself in an atmosphere of linguistic connotation whereby the path of gossip can be chosen over that relating important historical events. The events narrated within the text, the speaker's personal comments, his habit of letting his attention wander from the object he is describing and directing it squarely at the reader, the way in which the work is put together, and so forth, all point to the complex nature of Rodríguez Freile's work and explain the numerous frustrating attempts by "traditional" critics and literary historians to classify the work within a genre that best suits its structural characteristics.

Whatever the results of attempts to classify it according to genre, the importance of *El carnero* in the Hispanoamerican literary tradition lies in the original way in which it faces and tackles the reality depicted in the text. *El carnero* brought to New World literature maturity, confrontation, and awareness, such as the Spanish picaresque novel had brought to the Italianate humanist tendencies in the Peninsula. The novels *Lazarillo de Tormes* and *Guzmán de Alfarache* (Part 1, 1599) by

Mateo Alemán (1546–1614), or *Vida del buscón Don Pablos* [The Life of the Cheat Don Pablos] (1626) by Quevedo, depict the true historical and social reality of Spain, as opposed to the renaissance concept of literature as an imitation of idealized nature. Similarly, *El carnero* uncovers the true face of Hispanoamerican colonial society; it moves away from and thereby denies the norms of writing imposed on the officially approved "chronicles" that immediately preceded it. If *El carnero* cannot be classified as "literature" according to traditional Hispanic literary canons, it does, nevertheless, offer a form of writing as personal representation of reality that comes very close to poetic mimesis.

The social function of Rodríguez Freile's text is temporally and spatially similar to that adopted by literature in Spain during the second half of the sixteenth century. Referring to *Lazarillo de Tormes*, B. W. Wardropper, the English critic of Golden Age literature, stresses that its narrator was deliberately trying to show the seamy side of contemporary human existence. This is just the side that Balbuena, for example, does *not* show in *Grandeza mexicana*, or that Bramón embellishes with feeble pastoral images. At the beginning of the sixteenth century renaissance narrators had maintained a discrete silence about or idealized such aspects of life, as befitted the taste of their courtly readers. The purpose of the narrator of *Lazarillo*, on the other hand, as of the majority of picaresque novels, and, in fact, of works by authors of the second half of the sixteenth century in general, culminating in Cervantes's *Don Quixote*, is to show the side of society that earlier renaissance literature, with very rare exceptions such as *La Celestina*, had hidden, and to state categorically that social brilliance is only a disguising mask for human rapacity and that beauty is a cover for ugliness, to denounce, consciously or unconsciously, the deceitful play of appearances that constitutes the social dynamic in a period of historical misfortune and unrest.

In Hispanoamerica *El carnero* assumes the social responsibility common to much mannerist art and literature of its time. Superficially, the story line offered by Rodríguez Freile professes renaissance historiographic norms—it says that its purpose is to lend fame to the conquistadors and builders of the New Kingdom of Granada and to save its inhabitants from the shadow of oblivion—but the author had another, deeper objective to which he alludes in an offhand manner in the title and in the way in which the text is programed. This objective, of which the greater part of the narrative sequences of *El carnero* consists, was to show the hidden side of colonial society, the secret corners of colonial intrahistory dealt with in everyday gossip, and whose undoubted attraction for the narrator is masked by his tone of official disapproval. With intentions opposite to those of Balbuena, Rodríguez Freile writes of the naked reality beneath the placid, misleading social appearances in the colony.

As a result of the concept and function determining the narrative process of *El carnero*, the work shows a significant structural change from that of the traditional chronicle. For Rodríguez Freile, the written text is not analogous to spoken discourse, as early chroniclers evidently thought, but constitutes a particular type of communication whose validity and meaning are enclosed within the phenomenalistic frame of the written word. He is fully aware that the process of writing begets a book, an artifact destined for reading and for physical manipulation by the reader; *his* reader, therefore, must abandon the role of listener—which previous chroniclers had taken for granted—and assume an active responsibility, obeying the narrator's repeated exhortations. On telling of the customs of the Indians during the period of Cacique Guatavita before the arrival of the Spaniards, anticipating a possible reaction in the reader, he says:

> Paréceme que algún curioso me apunta con el dedo y me pregunta que de dónde supe estas antigüedades; pues tengo dicho que entre estos naturales no hubo quien escribiera, ni cronistas.

> It seems to me that some curious reader is going to point his finger at me and say "But how do you know these old things, if, as I understand, none of these natives could write, and there were no such things as chroniclers in those days?"

On another occasion the speaker is getting ready to tell about certain historical happenings between Cacique Guatavita and Cacique Bogotá; just in case the thread of the story has been lost, we are told "Now, reader, put your finger here and wait for me until I have finished telling about this war." Once he has finished the episode, he closes his parenthesis with a correlative sign of composition: "Now the reader can take his finger off the place where I told him to put it, because by now he will know what the ceremony is all about."

The conversion of the "passive listener" of the early chronicles of the Indies into the responsible collaborator demanded by Rodríguez Freile is, as a structural characteristic, congruent with the way in which the textual narrator stands out. *El carnero* is not innovative simply on account of its technique of telling the story from the point of view of an author who is at the same time narrator and witness to the facts, a form already extant in the realistic tradition of the Hispanoamerican eyewitness chronicle; its importance lies rather in the *change in outlook* of the narrator-witness, and in this respect it is typical of the great works of Hispanoamerican mannerism. The confidence in the power of human reason to organize and mete out internal justice, which was present during the conquest and domination of the New World, has disappeared, and in its place the speaker reveals an unstable, disenchanted Weltanschuung born of a feeling of irreparable loss, of awareness of living at a time in history similar to that known by the chronicler Suárez de Peralta, or found in the epic enunciation of Ercilla—that is to say, a period in which the values which had guided the conquest of the Indies have disappeared forever. During the time of Charles V, the narrator of *El carnero* tells us, there used to be a royal decree in the *Casa de Contratación* (Bureau of Commerce) in Seville stating that only those men (and their wives) whose family had been Christian for several generations could emigrate to the Indies: "This rule lasted for a long time, but the document must have been lost and now anybody can come." In another part of the discourse he explains that the decadence and insignificance of the New Kingdom of Granada are due to colonial bureaucrats paying no attention to the rules anymore—their decisions are purely arbitrary; meanwhile, the land has been impoverished by the insatiable rapacity of the Spanish who arrived at New Granada with no other intention but to return to Spain with riches.

In *El carnero* Rodríguez Freile creates the image of a narrator strongly pained by a feeling of having been deprived, usurped of what is rightfully his—a narrator who is the exact antithesis of the happy speaker in Balbuena's text who celebrates Hispanoamerica's role of tribute-payer. *El carnero* belongs with the great Hispanoamerican works of mannerism, not only in its awareness of difference informing the limits and rights of "us" and "them," but also in the combative, polemical attitude hidden behind the narrator's words. Along with *La Araucana*, Rodríguez Freile's "chronicle" is a taking off point for discussion of the main problems involved in the makeup of Hispanoamerican society. Like Ercilla, undecided between two opposing concepts of conquest, or the Inca Garcilaso, torn between allegiance to two homelands, the existential view in *El carnero* is of a speaker with a need to tell the truth and yet be obedient to moral dictates imposed on him. The disordered syntax of the writing, the dynamic multiplicity of his narrative enunciation, the parataxis of form, and so forth, are some of the immediate manifestations that reveal hidden tensions in the speaker's enunciative process, and these, while of mannerist origin, are nevertheless enclosed within the ideological framework imposed by the historical will to religious reintegration dominant during the baroque period in which Rodríguez Freile wrote his text. *El carnero* not only exposes with the utmost clarity the socio-historic conflicts of the time, but also endeavors to obey the ideological forces that tried to solve those conflicts by imposing religious dogma.

Undoubtedly, the predominant narrative interest in *El carnero* lies in descriptions of everyday colonial life itself, a level of existence that in the mannerist mode of representation has all the ambiguities of a comedy of errors. In spite of numerous moral interpolations interrupting the narrative stratum, any reader can intuit that the speaker has, in fact, little interest in divine matters but is drawn to those profane attractions formerly found on the human level of the cosmic medieval home. Non-narrative fragments of "preaching" abound but seem to lack authentic sincerity. In spite of what he says, the author is more attracted to telling a tale than to preaching moral fables; his true literary personality shows a preference for the ins and outs of colonial gossip rather than for correcting immoral behavior or bad habits.

Despite his true interests, the narrator of *El carnero* feels obliged to moralize. His story must comply with the exemplary purpose assigned to Hispanoamerican literature during the seventeenth century. This moralizing function need not necessarily be understood as an explicit restriction, although it was that too, but principally it was aimed at imposing the hegemonic outlook of reintegration following the religious upheavals of the historical period of the Reformation. The moralizing was to provide a frame of reference in which all historical elements would find a definitive meaning and purpose. Hence, in *El carnero*'s contradictory presentation of reality we see the conflict between past and present, between things as they are and as they should be, between the attraction of the here and now and the need for a universal morality. All these contradictions lead unequivocally to the structural law of the work, which lies in the conflict between the compulsive attraction of the profane for the writer and his obligation to deal with the transcendent dimension of existence.

The structure of *El carnero* then has to adapt itself to norms imposed by the reintegrating will in force during the seventeenth century by going against the speaker's implicit perspective. This ideological conjunction is found from the very beginning of the text, when the speaker declares his decision to write a history of the New Kingdom of Granada in homage to and gratitude toward his country. According to his own words, what has happened there cannot be compared with the conquests of Alexander the Great, the labors of Hercules, the deeds of Julius Caesar or Pompey, nor those of captains renowned for their bravery; nevertheless, and in spite of the historical insignificance of the conquest of New Granada, the event does not deserve to be hidden behind "shadows of oblivion." Although for its conquest "not many armies nor great forces were required, the country possesses great richness in its mineral veins, and from them great treasures have been taken away and removed to our Spain." Rodríguez Freile equates the prestige of the riches of New Grenada with the heroic deeds wrought in other lands, and thus raises his country's limited historical stature through the transforming process of writing, which is one of the "remedies" granted by God to human beings to "preserve the memory of the benefits received from His hand." The contradiction between the stated purpose in writing the text and the limited number of historical matters referred to in it is, then, explained away by placing the history of the New Kingdom of Granada within the universal plan for the salvation of mankind that God established from the beginning of time.

Having dedicated his first four chapters to events before the arrival of the Spaniards, and in particular to the story of the struggle between the Caciques Guatavita and Bogotá, surprisingly the speaker opens chapter 5 with the story of Satan's revolt and then goes on to tell the biblical story of Adam and Eve. The break in the narrative line is only superficial, however, and transgression of the lineality of the discourse is immediately justified:

> Paréceme que ha de haber muchos que digan: ¿qué tiene que ver la conquista del Nuevo Reino, costumbres y ritos de sus naturales, con los lugares de la Escritura y Testamento Viejo y otras historias antiguas? Curioso lector, respondo: que esta doncella es huérfana, y aunque hermosa y olvidada de todos, y porque es llegado el día de sus bodas y desposorio, para componerla es necesario pedir ropas y joyas prestadas, para que salga a vista; y de los mejores jardines coger las más agraciadas flores para la mesa de los convidados.

It seems to me that many of you will be saying "but what have the story of the conquest of New Granada and the laws and customs of its natives got to do with the writings of the Old Testament and other ancient stories?" To the curious reader I reply that this young lady is an orphan, and although she is beautiful, she has been forgotten by everyone. Now, because her wedding day has come, to remedy the situation it is necessary to borrow clothes and jewels to show her at her best, and to pick the most beautiful flowers from the best gardens to adorn the guests' tables.

The tying together of the two apparently different sequences is achieved as follows: after being thrown out of heaven, Lucifer was turned into the prince of this world, thanks to his triumph over Adam and Eve—a position he held until he was dethroned by Christ's redemption. However, since the Spanish, soldiers of the army of God, had not yet arrived at New Granada, Lucifer continued to reign among the inhabitants there:

> *antes que en este Reino entrase la palabra de Dios, es muy cierto que el demonio usaba de su monarquía, porque no quedó tan destituido de ella que no le haya quedado algún rastro, particularmente entre infieles y gentiles, que carecen del conocimiento del verdadero Dios; y estos naturales estaban y estuvieron en esta ceguedad hasta la conquista, por lo cual el demonio se hacía adorar de ellos, que le sirviesen con muchos ritos y ceremonias.*

before the word of God entered into this kingdom, it is very true that the Devil had his realm here, and he was never so completely banished from it that no trace of him remained, especially among infidels and non-Catholics who lack knowledge of the true God; and these natives remained in such darkness until the time of the conquest, and the Devil had made himself adored by them and they served him with many rites and ceremonies.

In this way the referent is adorned with the "borrowed clothes and jewels" of the biblical story; what happened in the New Kingdom of Granada cannot be understood if it is divorced from the divine rhythm of history.

Accommodating the narrative point of view to the intellectual schema of historical scholasticism determines the reappearance of a series of literary forms and recourse to discourse clearly dating back to the Middle Ages; for example, we find catalogs of historical names and precautionary commentaries for the reader's benefit, most of which, significantly, are attacks on woman—*arma del diablo, cabeza del pecado y destrucción del paraíso* ("the arm of the Devil, the head of sin, and the destroyer of Paradise")—and frequent biblical allusions, which serve the speaker's integrative purposes. This intellectual accommodation helped reinstate the popular medieval image of human life as a battlefield: all the incidents told in *El carnero* transmit in one way or another the idea of a social world where forces of angels fight against those of the Devil. For Rodríguez Freile this struggle did not end when the Spanish arrived in America but continued unabated in the society founded by those soldiers of Christ. The speaker uncovers in the nonheroic episodes dealing with colonial life in New Granada the presence of those same two forces in permanent dispute. The conquest of the New Kingdom has not ended in triumph for the soldiers of Christ. The permanent combat behind daily conflict is revealed in the social intrigues depicted in each episode of this comedy of errors; it exists in the very essence of Hispanoamerican social makeup. At first sight an incident might seem insignificant, but colonial gossip reveals the eternal struggle once again and thus forms a vital part, a new historical moment, in the divine plan of creation.

El carnero presents an existential conflict: Hispanoamerican man is seen as a being in strife, permanently subjected to contradictory forces. Paradoxically, by using post-Tridentine interpretive norms, Rodríguez Freile confirms propositions implicit in Hispanoamerican literature from its very beginnings: the image of human beings divided between desire and reality, between two ideals of justice, between two homelands, between the pull of the profane and a longing for the sacred. Time and time again we find conflictive and painful images even when, as has just been seen, the text is being made to adhere to the concept of cosmic order proposed by baroque literary norms. It is no accident that the speaker's attitude in *El carnero* should be ambiguous as he tells his tales. From the ethical point of view, Rodríguez Freile must condemn deviations from approved human conduct, but, in doing so, he cannot erase the impression that his true interest lies in the pleasure of bearing witness to those deviations rather than in the obligation to correct them through his writing.

THE RETURN TO THE ABANDONED HOME

It is not easy to establish clearly the moment of transition from mannerist to baroque tendencies. Contrary to the transition from romanesque to Gothic, or from renaissance to mannerist, full-bodied, even overblown, tendencies of representation and mannerist preferences continued unchanged throughout the baroque in the seventeenth century. In fact the conflicts frequently found in baroque representation of reality originated in the mannerist crisis of artistic vision that came into being when the renaissance hegemonic insistence on a belief in cosmic harmony began to be discredited and a radical ambiguity arose regarding a concept which had been considered firmly established. As a result, the mannerist image of reality in art involved an interplay of deceptive appearances.

Mannerist thought cannot truly be called a purely formal alteration of renaissance structures; the renaissance period of "classic" purity is not necessarily followed by a decadent period of "artifice"; literary tendencies are not necessarily devitalized and culturally silenced, as was previously believed by many historians and theorists of the arts. The mannerist period contains genuine expressivity and for the first time brings out into the open the system of conflicting forces which forms the basis of our modern outlook: pragmatic reason versus personal will, modern imperialism versus chivalric feudalism, the spirit of modern capitalism versus local barter and exchange. There arose an equivocal and contradictory spirit expressing irresolution and doubt, bourgeois individualism, the spirit of competition, the affirmation of human loneliness, social disenchantment, and an awareness that heroic values had been discredited.

In Hispanoamerica the assimilation of literary tendencies born of the mannerist spirit into the baroque ideological structure would indicate that there intellectual thought was, to some degree, ignorant of its roots. Even though mannerist and baroque literature have a completely different Weltanschauung, they do not differ basically one from the other as regards forms of expression. The mannerist writer sees Hispanoamerican space for the first time as a different reality, equivocal and unstable, and implies the difficulties inherent in understanding the meaning of existence in the New World; the mannerist recognizes the contradictory nature of Hispanoamerica that forms the very basis of its outlook. The baroque writer aims at solving the conflicts expressed in mannerist thought by adjusting the unstable mannerist image of reality to the rigorous schema of dogmatic, post-Tridentine Catholic thought. This latter attitude is revealed through complex attempts at reintegration—at times severe, at times routine—as exhibited in the works of authors such as Juan Ruiz de Alarcón (Mexico,

1580–Spain, 1639), Miguel de Guevara (Mexico, 1585?–1646?), Alonso de Ovalle (Chile, 1601–51), Francisco Núñez de Pineda (Chile, 1607–82), Matías de Bocanegra (Mexico, 1612–68), Carlos de Sigüenza y Góngora.

From its inception, Hispanoamerican thought was forged by a synthesis of dynamic polemical arguments, by the dialectic between the culture imported into the New World and subjected to the ideological pressures of a conflictive vision of reality, and the transforming circumstances of a world that appeared to offer unlimited possibilities. The meeting of Spanish culture and American environment produced a symbiotic relationship of considerable reach. The Spanish brought a sense of history and human behavior at variance with the philosophies of the more developed cultures of the New World; at first they had neither the time nor the interest to enter into a dialog with nor try to understand the indigenous world that presented itself to their astonished eyes. The process of transculturation, of a differentiating and renewing synthesis, however, began to affect them as soon as they had settled into their new home and came under the influence of a completely different reality from the one they had left behind.

In the second half of the sixteenth century, what could be called *criollo* expression proper came into being; this new, foreign interpretation shows that the corresponding forms retained in Peninsular literature had been significantly modified. From its beginnings Hispanoamerican literary discourse was conceived as reform-minded and polemical; its tradition was fired by the mannerist outlook inasmuch as this offered awareness of what was new, discarded previous interpretive systems, and asserted the differences. Hispanoamerican lyric poetry, inspired by the rhetorical schema of renaissance Europe, has a searing quality totally unknown in the Italianate lyrics of sixteenth-century Spain. Faced with the chronicles of the Indies written by historians who did not know firsthand the sources of American reality, the chroniclers who had been in America refuted the officially approved version of history and, through their own accounts, demanded a different understanding of Hispanoamerica—one impossible to attain within a European ideological framework. Theatrical performances, which were much used by priests to teach the Indians and which quickly became very popular, acquired, when performances depended on the Indians, a totally new tone from that of the drama in Spain.

In a classic book about Hispanoamerican culture (*De la Conquista a la Independencia* [From the Conquest to Independence], 1944)

Mariano Picón-Salas offers the hypothesis that the arrival of the Spanish in the New World prematurely destroyed a social evolution that would, perhaps, have developed into a system of large indigenous states, possibly culminating in one great united country—the same that Simón Bolívar (1783–1830) would fruitlessly dream of later. Something analogous occurred to intellectual thought in Hispanoamerica: recognition that different realities exist, which appears very early in Hispanoamerican literature, did not develop to even a minimum of its potential. Interest in the pre-Hispanic past appeared only after its destruction caused by the initial contact between the two worlds, and was accompanied by feelings of reintegration with the cosmic home of empire. If in the work of Terrazas, Ercilla, or the Inca Garcilaso a clear recognition of difference can be seen, in that of Balbuena, Diego de Hojeda, or Pedro de Oña the attitude is one of reintegration, and this, finally, dominated the literary and philosophic panorama of the colonies during the seventeenth and eighteenth centuries. After an initial blaze of glory in Hispanoamerican literature during the early and mannerist periods, the official hand of the empire, allied with the Church, clamped down on deviations from authorized lines, resulting in the generally less distinguished writings of the baroque.

Critics and historians of Hispanoamerican letters have clearly shown this intellectual backtracking—which, in Hispanoamerica, began near the start of the seventeenth century—to be the result of the will to establish the Spanish crown firmly in the New World, in the space of the cosmic home claimed by Spain in the face of the rest of European society. It is no accident that Balbuena, not satisfied with reassuring Spain of the tributary dependence of Mexico in his *Grandeza mexicana*, went on to write an epic poem singing the glories of the medieval Spanish hero Bernardo del Carpio; nor that Pedro de Oña and Hernando Domínguez Camargo chose to tell of the life of the Spanish Saint Ignatius Loyola. Something in common unites both epic characters beyond the distance of time and imagination—they personify two key moments of Spanish history: the rise of the Spanish political kingdom and its development into a worldwide messianic empire.

The very few novelistic writers who appear in Hispanoamerica at the beginning of the seventeenth century once again toe the line and avoid the risks of being different, preferring rather to take refuge in the comfortable security of the establishment. From the second half of the sixteenth century, Spain had been able to offer Hispanoamerica models of the modern novel, from the picaresque through *Don Quixote*. The turbulent attitude of polemic differentiation, upon which Hispanoamerican intellectual thought was founded, was, in fact, very close to the vigorous reformist strain in Spain and the powerful denunciation of social hypocrisy exemplified by the picaresque novels and by *Don Quixote*. Nevertheless, the very few existing early colonial novels, completely ignoring the forms that had started in Spain with *Lazarillo de Tormes* fifty years earlier, accommodate to the worn-out but hegemonically approved schemata of the pastoral novel rather than risk offending the powers that be. These early seventeenth-century Hispanoamerican novels have neither the structure nor the function of modern novels. They were created at a time when retrenchment held in check the sense of differentiation and identity visible in Hispanoamerican writing at the end of the sixteenth century, and instead of furthering the cause of reform and social criticism, are simply pastoral narratives dedicated to preaching and praising virtuous behavior. They do not risk awakening the suspicions of the viceregal authorities nor disturb the nascent bourgeois mentality of the New World.

The strength of this intellectual retrenching also explains the surprising popularity that lyric poetry in highly polished, stylized language acquired among seventeenth-century writers in the New World. We know from chroniclers that versifiers abounded in the streets of New Spain, and there are more than enough examples extant from the innumerable poetry competitions where *criollo* wits rivaled each other in allegorizing banal happenings from everyday colonial life. Both the nature of the early colonial pastoral novel and the abundant lyric poetry were consequences of the spirit of reintegration that dominated the period. Forbidden to express social criticisms, the poet preferred to use a form of discourse which, instead of depicting the true historical conditions of the surroundings, turned reality into artifice or an allegory of an abstract, sentimental, or insignificant nature.

In this aspect Hispanoamerica is intellectually close to Spain, where similar conditions had come to exist by the end of the seventeenth century. After the picaresque novels and *Don Quixote*, the modern novel languished and disappeared in the Peninsula, since its new techniques were prohibited under the new ideological imperatives. There too conditions eliminated any possibility of critical denunciation and ideological dissent. In colonial Hispanoamerica the results were even more dismal, delaying the appearance of the modern novel until the beginning of the nineteenth century; in place of the picaresque and *Quixote*, we find Góngora's poetic formulas, which Hispanoamerican literary discourse speedily mastered and applied ad nauseam. Much more than Lope de Vega, Quevedo, or Pedro Calderón de la Barca (1600–81), Góngora was the Peninsular model to be imitated, and Hispanoamerican poets identified with him to such a degree that many years after Góngora's death (in 1627) Juan de Espinoza Medrano (Peru, 1632–88), known as *"El lunarejo"* ("The Man with the Mole"), published his *Apologético en favor de don Luis de Góngora* [Apology in Favor of Don Luis de Góngora] (1662), a defense inspired by the distant imputations that one Don Manuel de Faría y Souza had directed at the work of Don Luis de Góngora of Córdoba, Spain.

The abundant Hispanoamerican "Gongorism" is a social rather than a literary phenomenon. *Criollo* poets generally took no notice of the social criticism in Góngora's work and imitated only the linguistic peculiarities his poetry offers. In this way they saw the work of Góngora as a lyric means of evading reality, as a model for writing in such a way as to develop a neutral intellectual expression that would not disturb the tranquility of the authorities in the quiescent colonial society. Early Hispanoamerican lyrics make language itself the object and meaning of poetic practice. The profound renovation of form that Góngora's lyrics had brought to Spanish poetry was converted into a rhetorical schema that, if not in every case, usually produced writing about the most insignificant facts of everyday colonial life or developed into linguistic juggling, making literary expression a banal game uncommitted to any immediate historical circumstances. In Hispanoamerica, Góngora became the model of how to say things without risking saying anything.

THE DIVINE REENCOUNTER

Approximately in the same period in which Gongoristic poetry began to be popular with the *criollo* wits of the New World, Padre José de Acosta (Spain, 1540–1600) returned to Spain after spending fifteen or sixteen years of his life on American soil. The chief result of his experience was the writing of *Historia natural y moral de las Indias* [A Natural and Moral History of the Indies], published in 1590. As he says in his Proem to the Reader, Padre Acosta wanted to write a different type of work—a history, but one not limited to describing surroundings or relating facts of the conquest. He wanted to make his text informative—telling about the lie of the land and natural characteristics of America and the history of its inhabitants—and analytical, explaining the causes for things found in those surroundings and the reasons for their historical behavior.

Padre Acosta was perfectly aware that his "history," due to the reasons stated above, would be somewhat unusual, and his writings are indeed very different from earlier historical narrations on the Indies:

> aunque el Mundo Nuevo ya no es nuevo sino viejo, según hay mucho dicho y escrito de él, todavía me parece que en alguna manera se podrá tener esta historia por nueva, por ser juntamente historia y en parte filosofía y por ser no sólo de las obras de naturaleza, sino también de las del libre albedrío, que son los hechos y costumbres de los hombres.

> although the New World is not so new anymore but is, rather, old, because much has been said and written about it; still, it seems to me, that in some way this history can be considered new, because it is at the same time part history and part philosophy, not only about actual works of nature, but also about free will, and facts and customs of men.

From this we get the unusual title he gives his text, which, although strange at first sight, can be well understood according to his explanation; it is "natural" history in descriptions of things of nature, and "moral" because it covers philosophical aspects and free will—subjects never taken into consideration by other chroniclers of the Indies.

Padre Acosta's explicit declaration about the new nature of his writing brings him close to the mannerist thinkers of the sixteenth century. He carefully refrains from furthering, with his words, any system of norms to uphold a concept of reality; his purpose in writing is not, as the renaissance writers had artistically stated, to imitate nature, but rather to reveal, with the help of the creative and investigative word, a different vision of reality by uncovering hidden meanings.

The awareness of "the new" shown in the *Historia natural y moral de las Indias* is, however, also subordinated to the attitude of ideological reintegration, which finally proves to be the true purpose guiding the text. The dimensions of difference and reintegration are fixed in the proem. Padre Acosta insists, as we see from the preceding quotation, that his interpretation of reality is "new," and he goes on in the subsequent three sentences to establish three purposes for his history, all of which form part of heavenly design:

El fin de este trabajo es, que por la noticia de las obras naturales que el Autor tan sabio de toda naturaleza ha hecho, se le dé alabanza y gloria al Altísimo Dios, que es maravilloso en todas partes. Y por el conocimiento de las costumbres y cosas propias de los indios, ellos sean ayudados a conseguir y permanecer en la gracia de la alta vocación del Santo Evangelio, al cual se dignó en el fin de los siglos traer gente tan ciega, el que alumbra desde los montes altísimos de su eternidad. Ultra de eso podrá cada uno para sí, sacar también algún fruto, pues por bajo que sea el sujeto, el hombre sabio saca para sí sabiduría y de los más viles y pequeños animalejos se puede tirar muy alta consideración y muy provechosa filosofía.

The purpose of this work is that through news of the natural works of the all-wise Author of all nature, praise and glory be given to Him, the Most High God, who is marvelous in all places. And by knowledge of the customs and things native to the Indians, they might be helped to obtain the grace of the high vocation of the Sacred Gospel, and to remain therein; for that which illuminates from the highest mountains of His eternity is vouchsafed after centuries to be brought to a people most blind. And furthermore, each [reader] might obtain some fruit for himself also, since, however lowly the subject, man can gain wisdom from it; from the smallest and lowliest of the animals can be drawn high consideration and very fruitful philosophy.

Padre Acosta presents his three purposes in decreasing order of importance and the last—to add to the knowledge of nature—is the least important of the three objectives; furthering the conversion of the Indians through better understanding of their customs is the second. The first and most important, which doubtless incorporates the two others, is to inspire the reader to praise and glorify God, the author of the natural wonders to be described in the text following the proem. Padre Acosta's work is described by him as an instrument for the greater honor and glory of God. The true purpose of the *Historia natural y moral de las Indias* is transcendent. We clearly see the nature of the "new" character attributed to it by the author; unlike previous chronicles and histories whose specific function was simply to inform the reader, Padre Acosta's work has an ethical, a religious function—to lead the reader, through knowledge of the natural marvels created by God, to find and praise the Creator.

THE SADDER BUT WISER RETURN

The return of sinners to their Creator seldom takes place in an atmosphere of Christian joy, but rather through contrition and repentance. One of the characteristic motifs appearing in Hispanoamerican colonial literature is "the sadder but wiser return." Sinners recognize their condition as such, how they have strayed from God and fallen into evil ways; at the same time they confess in anguish their human weakness and their powerless efforts to return unaided to their abandoned home:

> *Levántame, Señor, que estoy caído,*
> *sin amor, sin temor, sin fe, sin miedo;*
> *quiérome levantar, y estoyme quedo;*
> *yo propio lo deseo y yo lo impido.*
> *Estoy, siendo un sólo, dividido;*
> *a un tiempo muero y vivo, triste y ledo;*
> *lo que puedo hacer, eso no puedo;*
> *huyo del mal y estoy en él metido.*
> *Tan obstinado estoy en mi porfía,*
> *que el temor de perderme y de perderte*
> *jamás de mi mal uso me desvía.*
> *Tu poder y tu bondad truequen mi suerte*
> *que en otros veo enmienda cada día*
> *y en mí nuevos deseos de ofenderte.*

> Raise me, O Lord, for I am fallen,
> without love, without faith, without fear;
> I would arise alone, and I am still;
> I myself desire it, yet impede it.
> I am one and yet divided; at once
> I die and live, am sad and joyful.
> That which I could do, I do not;
> I flee from evil yet live within it.
> So stubbornly I persevere [in sinning]
> that fear of losing myself and Thee
> never turns me from my evil ways.
> Thy power and grace might change my fortune,

as I see others' improved each day,
while in me rise new wishes to offend Thee.

In this sonnet by Miguel de Guevara, the speaker shows a typical mannerist outlook; he recognizes and admits his divided nature and the conflicting opposites that violate his original spiritual unity. He wears himself out and weakens from living in a permanent state of unresolved tensions, and his only possibility of salvation is through divine help; the force of God alone can take him back to the home he cannot otherwise reach.

The motif of the return of the prodigal appears in different variants in the literature of Spain and Hispanoamerica. Probably the best known text in this sense is the sonnet by the Spaniard Lope de Vega, in which the original lost space is explicitly identified with a homeland:

Cuando me paro a contemplar mi estado
y a ver los pasos por donde he venido,
me espanto de que un hombre tan perdido
a conocer su error haya llegado.
Cuando miro los años que he pasado
la divina razón puesta en olvido,
conozco que piedad del cielo ha sido
no haberme en tanto mal precipitado.
Entré por laberinto tan extraño
fiando al débil hilo de la vida
el tarde conocido desengaño;
mas de tu luz mi oscuridad vencida,
el monstruo muerto de mi ciego engaño
vuelve a la patria, la razón perdida.

When I pause to contemplate my state
and look back at the steps whereby I've come,
I am terrified that a man so lost
can come to know the error of his ways.
And when I view the years that I have spent
oblivious to divine reason,
I know it was by the mercy of Heaven
that I did not fall into such evil.
I entered through so strange a labyrinth,

trusting to the weak thread of life
to reach enlightenment, too late acknowledged;
but Thy light vanquished my darkness,
dead the monster of my blind deceit,
lost reason returns to its homeland.

The signs of the motif are always present: the speaker recognizes himself as an irredeemable sinner and declares his absolute confidence in
heavenly goodness and forgiveness. It appears again in the work of
the later Hispanoamerican baroque writers, such as Juan del Valle
Caviedes (Spain, ca. 1652–Peru, ca. 1698):

> Congojado mi espíritu cobarde,
> vergonzoso y confuso, llega a veros,
> que, aunque mucho he tardado en conoceros,
> tengo un Dios como Vos para que aguarde.
> El jornalero soy que, por la tarde,
> llegó a la viña donde otros jornaleros
> que madrugaron más, tantos dineros
> les disteis como a aquél que llegó tarde.
> Mi maldad, mi desgracia y mi pecado,
> de quien soy me han tenido siempre ajeno,
> teniéndos con los vicios olvidado,
> ciego en torpezas, de miserias lleno,
> mas para pecador tan obstinado
> hay un Dios infinitamente bueno.

Anguished, my coward spirit,
shameful and confused, arrives to see Thee,
though I have delayed too long in knowing Thee,
I have such a God as Thou art, awaiting.
I am the laborer who arrived at the vineyard
in the afternoon, while other workers
rose at dawn; yet Thou gavest the same
to him who arrived late.
My evil, my disgrace, and my sin,
have held me at a distance from myself;
through my vice have I forgotten Thee;

blind with foolishness, filled with wretchedness,
even for a sinner so persistent
there is an infinitely good God.

The motif of the prodigal's return to his abandoned home precisely determines the structure of the two most important narrative works of the second half of the seventeenth century: *El pastor de Nochebuena* [The Christmas Shepherd], by Bishop Juan de Palafox, and *Infortunios de Alonso Ramírez* [Misfortunes of Alonso Ramírez] by Carlos de Sigüenza y Góngora.

Juan de Palafox, bishop of the diocese of Puebla in New Spain (Mexico) between 1640 and 1649, conceived his work *El pastor de Nochebuena* (1644) as edifying reading for the nuns in his jurisdiction. As he himself says, he preferred to write an allegorical narrative as being more likely to avoid "the tedium with which fragile natures receive spiritual treatises," and to make the ethical didactic function of the text more effective for his female readers! As indicated by the title, the book is set near Christmastime, when a shepherd has a dream in which he is taken back to the time and place of the birth of Christ. From there he begins a long tour through an imaginary space inhabited by virtues and vices. Finally, he returns to his own original home with the wisdom needed to carry out in exemplary fashion his responsibility as a shepherd.

The baroque outlook had again given literature an ethical function, and reality is represented by allegory, as Palafox says in his Introduction to the tale:

> *Este modo de explicarse por figuras que la Escritura llama parabólico, es no sólo muy común en la erudición profana, sino en la misma sagrada; antes bien, tanto más en ésta, cuanto la grandeza y profundidad del sentido necesita de más cuidado y fuerza en su explicación, para que pueda el ingenio humano, limitado y corto, penetrar en cuanto se le concede a nuestra fragilidad, tantos y tan celestiales misterios como se encierran en ella.*

> This method of explaining by figures, which Holy Writ calls "parable," is not only very common in profane letters, but also in those which are holy; in earlier times, and especially today when greatness and profundity of meaning needs even more care and force in its explanation, so that limited and short

human intelligence can penetrate, insofar as our frailty allows it, so many and so holy mysteries as are enclosed within it.

The shepherd is a symbolic figure of humanity, dedicated to leading souls, and with all the contradictions and doubts native to the mannerist personality. On contemplating the newborn Christ, the shepherd asks his divine help to free him from the blindness in which he lives, since, he says, "footsore, I am obliged to walk; afflicted, I seek consolation; and pursued, support." His lamentations are heard by an angel who offers help because angels are shepherds of men, whom they guide and defend, just as shepherds are angels to the sheep. The problem afflicting the shepherd is the characteristic conflict of mannerist literature: the loneliness and helplessness, the permanent tribulations and confused knowledge, which make humanity incapable of distinguishing between what is true and what is false:

> *Fáltame la luz con que, sin los primeros principios de los remedios, veo sin remedio los daños. Ando buscando lo bueno y no lo encuentro; ando huyendo de lo malo, y luego lo hallo. ¿Si no puedo conocer, Angel Santo, podré obrar, siendo el conocimiento el primero y más eficaz paso del acierto?*

> I lack the light with which to seek help; without it I see only dangers. I look for good and do not find it; I flee from evil and I find it indeed. Holy Angel, how can I know how to act, knowledge being the first and best step to certainty?

If the shepherd's words reflect the conflicts of man, the angel's reply embodies the diagnosis that the post-Tridentine Catholic Church wanted to be the definitive solution:

> *Tu daño, amigo, está en no acabar de conocer las cosas como son, pues es de creer que en tu profesión y obligaciones, en llegando a conocerlas con la divinia gracia, seguirá la voluntad la luz del entendimiento. Hasta ahora no has hecho jornada a las virtudes, ni llegado a conocer perfectamente los vicios. De aquí te resultan dos daños de gran ruina, que son: el no amar con ansia lo que te conviene, ni apartarte con aversión bastante de lo que te daña.*

> Your danger, my friend, is in not getting to know things as they really are; I imagine that with your work and responsibilities, in coming to know them through divine grace, you will choose the

path of light and understanding. Until now, you have not done a day's work in virtue, nor have you come to recognize the vices. From this come the two great dangers of your downfall, which are: not loving with fervor that which you should, nor fleeing with sufficient aversion that which is harmful.

The meeting with the heavenly guide is the initial sequence in an archetypal journey to obtain a prize; in the case of Palafox's text, the prize is wisdom, thus teaching the reader to distinguish between virtues and vices, to love the first and to hate the second. The shepherd's journey is structured on a systematic series of meetings with characters who symbolize vices and virtues, and finally, in the "Street of Time," the shepherd learns the Only Truth:

> *Todo es contrario a lo que parece, parece consejo y es engaño; parece diamante y es vidrio; parece hermosura y es corrupción; parece vida y es muerte.*

All is contrary to what it appears; what appears to be good advice is deception; what appears to be a diamond is glass; what appears as beauty is corruption; what seems to be life is death.

Once having obtained the final gift, the shepherd, transformed into a different being from the one who started the pilgrimage, returns to his sheep. Knowledge of Christian truth has banished his old afflictions. Now he knows that the earthly space of the cosmic home is, in truth, a place of deceit and error, of lies and pretense. Nothing has changed in the world; it is still changeable and capricious, deceitful and transitory, but the truth the shepherd has gained is his most effective weapon to conquer the risks arising from ignorance.

Infortunios de Alonso Ramírez was published in 1690 by Sigüenza y Góngora, who, with Sor Juana Inés de la Cruz (Mexico, 1648–95) and del Valle y Caviedes, is among the most interesting figures of the late Hispanoamerican baroque period. *Infortunios* is a key text in the colonial narrative. In it the historic and the imaginary are intertwined, since Sigüenza, perhaps consciously, tried to place a protective veil over the subject of his narration. More important than establishing the source from which Sigüenza obtained his material is the way in which the narrative has been organized; this gives it undeniable literary value.

The story in *Infortunios* is a simple one: Alonso Ramírez, born in Puerto Rico, leaves home at the age of thirteen to better his lot. He goes to Mexico, then later, on his way to the Philippines, is captured by English privateers (known to the readers of Spanish as "pirates"). After they finally free him, he lands in Yucatan and from there returns to Mexico City, where he meets Sigüenza, who listens to the tale of his travels and writes down the text.

The narrative technique in the composition of the tale, as with *El pastor de Nochebuena*, is that known in English as the "cervantene motif"—namely, the "framed" story within a story, in which a basic narrator tells what someone told him or gave to him in writing. In Palafox's text, chapter 1 ends with the angel inviting the shepherd to journey with him. According to the basic narrator, the shepherd himself "when he returned from his travels told me all that had happened, and in the following words." The end of the discourse closes the narrative frame, which had started with chapter 2, and states:

> *Esto me dijo que le sucedió al pastor en aquella Santa Noche, y yo, luego que lo oí, lo encomendé a la memoria y escríbilo por si hubiese alguno que desde ella quisiera pasarlo a la voluntad.*

> So the shepherd told me of all that happened to him on that Holy Night, and I, after hearing it, committed it to memory and wrote it down in case anyone should wish to benefit from it.

In *Infortunios*, at the end of the text the reader is informed that Alonso Ramírez was sent by the viceroy to Sigüenza, who, taking pity on him for the misfortunes he had undergone on his travels, helped him by formally writing down a report of his story in order to file a complaint against those in Yucatan and Mexico City who were attempting to defraud him; the last page of the text tells us that the report was successful in getting Alonso his due. By the author's adopting this frame, in which he is ostensibly simply transcribing a report on the orders of the viceroy, he is able to include a strong denunciation of the condition to which Mexican society had fallen, without taking on the responsibility and the risk of the opinions being his own.

The use of the framed narrative is different in the two cases under discussion. In *El pastor de Nochebuena* the frame is used to give verisimilitude to an edifying tale propagandizing Christian virtues. In *Infortunios*, on the other hand, a different kind of verisimilitude is being sought, primarily due to the different natures of the two tales. Fifty critical and decisive years had passed since Palafox's text was published, during which the Christian confidence it shows had given way to a new attitude, which, while generally adhering to the customary lines of baroque thought, shifted its interest to the immediate concrete problems of the common man. Explanations—semispiritual and semiscientific—of material phenomena, and the spiritual search for a feeling of belonging, had replaced the concept of the divine universal home of European baroque understanding.

The new character of narrative intent in *Infortunios* is explicitly set forth in the first paragraph of the text. This narrative, it says, will offer elements of both pleasure and of benefit, but

> *no será esto lo que yo aquí intente, sino solicitar lástimas que, aunque posteriores a mis trabajos, harán por lo menos tolerable su memoria, trayéndolas a compañía de las que me tenía a mí mismo cuando me aquejaban.*

> that will not be my main aim here, but rather to inspire the reader's pity, which, although subsequent to my work, will at least make tolerable the memory of it, causing the same feelings that I had when I heard the story.

Infortunios aims at moving the reader; it is a story to inspire solidarity arising from mutually felt pity on considering the sufferings of a fellow human being. Within the narrative code this purpose was fulfilled with the first intended reader—the viceroy—who had sent Ramírez to tell his tale of woe to Sigüenza; this, moreover, justifies the framing of the story. Sigüenza then decides to write up the story of the unfortunate Ramírez, since he pities him for all he has suffered.

It is not only at the story level that the work is destined to move its readers. Sigüenza's discourse arouses his readers' pity for Ramírez and also reveals the irreversible downfall of the society in which the misfortunes occurred. The space of the fiction appears to be seen in the baroque manner, as a battlefield between positive and negative forces, except that it is not only the English "pirates" who personify evil, but—and this is the key to the whole work—Spanish colonial society itself. At the end of the seventeenth century Spain was no longer the proud and victorious kingdom it had been under Charles V or Philip II, nor were the colonies the dynamically vigorous places of before. As background to Alonso's adversities, we clearly see the image of a foundering empire that has lost its old power, is besieged and terrified by the "heretic" privateers who sail up and down its coasts with impunity, and is consumed from within by the members of the society itself.

In *Infortunios de Alonso Ramírez* the motif of the return to the home that had been left behind takes on a completely different ideological tone (it is obviously immaterial that Alonso Ramírez came from Puerto Rico and returns at the end to Mexico, since his position is that of a person of Spanish descent moving inside and outside the Spanish world). The cosmic home no longer gives protection or guardianship against the outside world. The home to which return is sought has lost its sheltering roof. In the first part of the story, Ramírez suffers countless hardships in Mexico. In the second, we learn of his misfortunes at the hands of the Protestant English privateers. In the third part Ramírez returns to the Hispanic world and finds that his misfortunes continue: now he is caught by the ambitions and bureaucratic red tape tied up by the *criollos* themselves.

In each of the three sequences Alonso Ramírez plays the role of captive victim. In the first he lacks the economic means to juggle the possibilities that exist in a *criollo* world; in the second he is the victim of the satanic cruelty of the enemies of Spain; and in the third he is attacked by the corrupt colonial bureaucracy. His condition as victim is the distinctive sign of his existence; this is his motive for deciding at the end of the first part to embark for the Philippines:

> *Desesperé entonces de poder ser algo y hallándome en el tribunal de mi propia conciencia no sólo acusado, sino convencido de inútil, quise darme por pena de este delito la que se da en México a los que son delincuentes, que es enviarlos desterrados a las Filipinas.*

> I despaired then of ever getting to be anything, and finding myself not only guilty before the jury of my own conscience but also useless, I decided to punish myself as the Mexicans punish their guilty criminals by banishing them to the Philippines.

Alonso Ramírez in this way assumes the role of the modern hero; his characteristic outline is made obvious through the disillusioned attitude of the narrator who forms his audience. He is the individual who, by living in an unprotected space, discovers that the crime of existing must, by one means or another, be expiated.

Sigüenza y Góngora's text illustrates an undoubted weakening of the powerful political and religious spirit of conviction that characterized baroque literature before it. The social deterioration shown in the three parts of the tale is an unmistakable symptom of a moment of historical decline. Spain is failing, and with it all the system of reasoning that it had managed to impose on its colonies. The fear that the *criollos* feel of the English "heretics," and their impotence when faced with the new power of the bureaucrats, with all the disenchantment and afflictions that these attitudes imply, lead to events appearing to happen by chance even though the narrator's discourse pays occasional lip service to the official view of a divinely ordained world to the extent of presenting what shows as a false front. The adventures of Alonso Ramírez provide the most authentic, heart-rending account of the fall of an empire, put into the mouth of a disillusioned, skeptical descendant of the conquistadors; his discourse must still, however, adhere to the stale linguistic formulas of dull authority.

A WORLD OF LIGHTS AND SIGNS

Baroque art, Arnold Hauser affirms, produces a special thrill in the observer who beholds the concept of infinite yet integrated cosmic space. Hispanoamerican baroque literature fostered a reunion between the human being and God in the security of the cosmic Christian home, but the one who returned home, sadder but wiser, did not return to the same mental space left behind. The medieval image of the "good house" had given way to a cosmic concept of infinite dimensions: God does not dwell outside the human abode; His power and presence radiate from the interior of man's home itself:

> *¿Dónde pondré, Señor, mis tristes ojos*
> *que no vea tu poder divino y santo?*
> *Si al cielo los levanto,*
> *del sol en los ardientes rayos rojos*
> *te miro hacer asiento;*
> *si al manto de la noche soñoliento,*
> *leyes te veo poner a las estrellas;*
> *si los bajo a las tiernas plantas bellas,*
> *te veo pintar flores;*
> *si los vuelvo a mirar, los pecadores*
> *que tan sin rienda viven como vivo,*
> *con amor excesivo,*
> *allí hallo tus brazos ocupados,*
> *más en sufrir que en castigar pecados.*

Where shall I direct, O Lord, my sad eyes
that I not see Thy divine and holy power?
If I raise them to the skies,
I can see Thee making a place
for the sun amidst ardent burning rays;
if under the mantle of drowsy night,
I see Thee giving laws to the stars;
if I lower them to the tender lovely plants,
I see Thee paint the flowers;
if I turn to look again, sinners
who live as unbridled as I,
with excessive love
there I find held in Thine arms,
more in suffering sins than punishing.

This psalm by the Spanish writer Francisco de Quevedo admirably reveals a divine universe with which baroque literature proposed to replace the image of the silent God discovered by the mannerists. A new cosmic awareness revitalizes the figurative representation of reality, but the aesthetic effect of Quevedo's text is not to provoke a sentiment of placid, perfect order, as in medieval depictions of nature, but a "numinous" or spiritually elevated effect that the art historian, Werner Weisbach, in his commentary on Rudolf Otto, calls "the primary emotion of the divine as that beyond all rationality." In Catholic baroque art this "thrill of infinity" is closely allied to the concept of a boundless divinity: the world is filled with the Lord God; human beings do not need any mysterious ecstasy to transport them to His presence, since everyday reality itself is full of miracles. Simply by observing everything around us attentively we will find that natural objects are the permanent, indestructible manifestations of the glory of divine power.

The new way of viewing the cosmos, integrative and pantheistic at the same time, requires that we see the world as ordered by God on a monumental scale and calls into play a complex system of clues whose literary function is to caution and remind us of the permanent subordination of human conduct to God's will. Hispanoamerican baroque discourse, whatever its specific nature, was always directed at reinstalling God in the human home and in relating immediate concrete forms of daily life to the divinely ordained supernatural structure. The "divine encounter" became another characteristic situation represented in this discourse—a motif found in different forms throughout the seventeenth and eighteenth centuries, culminating in the work of the Abbé Manuel Lacunza (Chile, 1731–1801), *La venida del Mesías en gloria y majestad* [The Coming of the Messiah in Glory and Majesty] (1790; published 1811), foretelling the reign of Christ on earth and revealing the last throes of baroque thought at the time the new but yet tenuous intellectual strain of the Enlightenment was arising in Hispanoamerica.

The reintegrative function that characterizes Hispanoamerican baroque literature took the sting from the innovations inherited from works of the mannerist generation. Padre Acosta devotes chapter 10 of Book 3 of his *Historia natural* to a description of the seas that surround the Americas and mentions the opinion held by some that there is a need for a canal through Panama to unite the two oceans, thus making the trip to Peru much easier. He gives reasons for scientific opposition to the project:

> *A esta plática no falta quien diga que sería anegar la tierra, porque quieren decir que el un mar está más bajo que el otro, como en tiempos pasados se halla por las historias haberse dejado de continuar por la misma consideración el Mar Rojo con el Nilo, en tiempo del rey Sesostris, y después del Imperio Otomano.*

> In this discussion there is no lack of those who believe the land would be flooded because, they say, one ocean is lower than the other, as in times past there were the same considerations about the Red Sea and the Nile, in the time of King Sesostris, and afterward, the Ottoman empire.

Padre Acosta goes on to explain that in his personal judgment, however, the real impediment to the project is that human beings do not have the right or authority to alter the way in which God has made the world. To trample on His divine plan, which holds things together in the way they are, would be a punishable offense in the eyes of the Creator:

> *Mas para mí tengo por cosa vana tal pretensión, aunque no hubiese el inconveniente que dice, el cual yo no tengo por cierto; pero esto para mí que ningún poder humano bastará a derribar el monte fortísimo e impenetrable que Dios puso entre los dos mares, de montes y peñas*

durísimas que bastan a sustentar la furia de ambos mares. Y cuando fuese a hombres posible, sería a mi parecer muy justo temer del castigo del cielo querer enmendar las obras que el Hacedor, con sumo acuerdo y providencia, ordenó en la fábrica de este universo.

I personally hold such pretentions as vain, even if there were not the problem that they talk about, of which I am not entirely sure; however, for me, no human power will be enough to lay low the impenetrable mountain that God has placed between the two seas—mountains and rocks strong enough to hold back the fury of both the seas. And if it were for me to say, it would be quite right to fear the punishment of Heaven for trying to correct the works of the Creator, which He arranged with great providence and accord when making this universe.

An excellent illustration of the way in which Hispanoamerican baroque literature handles the motif of the divine encounter is found in the *Histórica relación del Reino de Chile* [History of the Kingdom of Chile] (1646), by Padre Alonso de Ovalle. Ovalle's perspective transforms the world of objects into a divine superreality: man's home is God's home at one and the same time. When the speaker in the *Histórica relación* describes the cordillera of the Andes, he aims much further than merely producing an aesthetic effect on the reader; the image of the cordillera is meant to put the reader in contact with God:

lo que he visto muchas veces es que cuando, después de algún buen aguacero que suele durar dos y tres y más días, se descubre esta cordillera (porque todo el tiempo que dura el agua está cubierta de nublados), aparece toda blanca desde su pie hasta las puntas de los primeros y anteriores montes que están delante, y causa una hermosísima vista, porque es el aire de aquel cielo tan puro y limpio, que, pasado el temporal, aunque sea en lo más riguroso del invierno lo despeja de manera que no aparece en él una nube ni se ve en muchos días; y entonces, rayando el sol en aquella inmensidad de nieves y en aquellas empinadas laderas y blancos costados y cuchillas de tan dilatadas sierras, hacen una vista que aun a los que nacemos allí y estamos acostumbrados a ella, nos admira y da motivos de alabanzas al Criador, que tal belleza pudo crear.

what I have seen many times is when, after a good rain, which lasts two or three days as a rule, the cordillera reappears (during the time the rains last it is hidden by clouds) covered in white from the foot to the peaks of the first front range, producing a most beautiful view, because the air and the sky are so pure and clean that—the storm being over—not a cloud is seen, even if it is the harshest winter day, and it remains unclouded for many days. Then, with the sun shining on that expanse of snow and on the sloping white sides and knife edges of those numerous peaks, it is a view that even those of us who were born there and are used to it must stop and look and admire, and praise the Creator who can make something so beautiful. [Book 1, chapter 5]

And it is not only the grandiose that shows God's presence; He is also to be found in the depths of the sea. Speaking of a shellfish, Ovalle says:

Otro género de mariscos se llama mañegües, *y está encerrado en dos conchas redondas, de la figura de los que sirven de modelo para los nichos de los retablos. La comida de dentro es más gruesa y no de tanta estima, pero de gran sustento. En cierta especie de este género, que son más pequeños, abriendo la concha, que es por de dentro como de madre-perla, y sacando la comida, se ve estampado dentro de ella un contorno de color morado, parecido al de una imagen de la Virgen Santísima con su manto y el niño en los brazos, que causa gran consuelo y devoción, y aunque se representa esto en todas las conchas de esta especie, pero en algunas es con tan primor que admira.*

Another type of shellfish that we call *mañegües*, consists of two round shells closed together, just like the one used as a model for niches in altar pieces. The part you eat is inside the thickest half; it is nothing out of the ordinary, but still quite good to eat. In a certain species of this genus—the very tiny ones—you open the shell and inside it is as mother-of-pearl, and as you take out the flesh that you eat, you see that the shell is colored purplish inside, so it is just like the image of the Holy Virgin with her cloak and the Child in her arms, which brings great consolation and devotion. And although you can see it in all the shells of the species, in some it is so clear that it takes your breath away. [Book 1, chapter 16]

Referring to the trees of Chile, Ovalle tells of the discovery of a particularly interesting one—a tree that looks so realistically like the crucified Christ that the bishop of Santiago has granted indulgences to anyone who goes to see it. The bishop *quedó admirado y consolado de ver un tan grande y nuevo argumento de nuestra fe, que como comienza en aquel Nuevo Mundo a echar sus raíces, quiere el Autor de la naturaleza que las de los mesmos árboles broten y den testimonio de ellas, no ya en jeroglíficos, sino en la verdadera representación de la muerte y pasión de nuestro Redentor.*

was astonished and consoled to see such a great new argument in favor of our faith, which, as it is beginning to put down its roots in the New World, the Author of Nature wants the trees themselves to come forth and bear witness, not in hieroglyphics, but in true representation of the passion and death of our Redeemer.

The tree, then, is a sign that leads people to the divine presence, as do the cordillera and the *mañegües*. Later, when speaking of his personal knowledge of the marvelous tree, Ovalle's words unmistakably describe an experience of the numinous:

Yo confieso de mí que luego que de los umbrales de la iglesia vi este prodigioso árbol, y a la primera vista se me representó en un todo confuso aquella celestial figura del crucifijo, me sentí movido interiormente y como fuera de mí, reconociendo a vista de ojos lo que apenas se puede creer si no se ve, ni yo había pensado que era tanto aunque me lo habían encarecido como se merece.

I confess that when from the threshhold of the church I saw this extraordinary tree, even though at first sight it only appeared indistinctly like the heavenly figure of the crucifix, I nonetheless felt stirred to the depths of my being, disembodied, and I could scarcely believe what my eyes were seeing, nor did I think that it had been exaggerated more than it deserves.

The most important aspect of Ovalle's writing is not his personal experience per se, but the way in which he tries to inspire in his readers a thrill similar to his own when considering the incarnate divinity:

Por esto no me he contentado de referir esto en este escrito, sino que he querido añadir juntamente un estampa, que es la que se ve en la hoja siguiente y está ajustada con su original todo lo posible, para que el piadoso lector tenga en qué admirar la divina sabiduría de nuestro Dios y su altísima providencia en los medios y motivos que nos ha dado, aun en las cosas naturales e insensibles, para confirmación de nuestra fe y aumento de la piedad y devoción de sus fieles.

For this reason I have not been content simply to refer to this in writing; I have added a sketch, which can be seen on the next page, fashioned like the original as much as possible, so that the pious reader can admire the divine wisdom of God and His most high providence in the means and motifs that he has given us, even in natural and insensate things, to confirm our faith and increase the piety and devotion of the faithful. [Book 1, chapter 23]

The motivation behind Alonso de Ovalle's propaganda for Chile, is, after all, of an ethical and religious character. Chile is presented by him as a privileged or chosen land because nature there is a vehicle that constantly takes us to the divine presence. The sensuousness of his style serves the spiritual purpose of his writing. His pleasure in creating a true-to-life impression of Chilean natural wonders is based on the baroque idea that these are cosmic signs that convert human existence into a happy, sustained metaphysical state of excitement.

If for Ovalle the cordillera, sea, and woods of his country are signs of the ever-living presence of God among men, for Hernando Domínguez Camargo the beauties of the surroundings are signs that teach men of the deadly consequences of misbehavior. In his most famous poem, *"A un salto por donde se despeña el arroyo de Chillo"* ["To a waterfall where the stream of Chillo descends from a rock"], the speaker uses metaphors in the style of Góngora: the image of the river as a colt that runs arrogantly along its streambed; in its pride it does not heed where it is going, grows prouder all the time until it hits a rocky shelf, and, as a result, falls crashing into the abyss. The speaker's poetic mastery is indisputable, but the text makes no attempt to impress the reader with poetic artistry for its own sake; rather, it strives to teach a moral lesson about the dangers of the misguided life. The aesthetic function of the poem is subordinate to the ethical, summed up in the final verse:

> *Escarmiento es de arroyuelos*
> *que se alteran fugitivos,*
> *porque así amansan las peñas*
> *a los potros cristalinos.*

> Let this be a lesson to streams
> bounding wildly on their way,
> for rocks are there to tame
> those bright, shining colts.

The baroque concept of reality in literature is not a return to the harmonious universe proposed by renaissance writers. As we have said, the baroque thinkers emphasize reality as the same interplay of deceptive appearances that so disturbed the mannerists, but problems of fear, the risk of confusion, anguish at the possibility of being deceived, and helplessness when faced with ambiguity can be solved through the use of religious revelation. Baroque literature teaches that although human beings are constantly exposed to the danger of damning themselves through error, they can also obtain considerable help in clearing up their confusion through those guiding elements that God places in their path. The only ones who stand condemned with all certainty are those who willfully refuse to listen to advice and to heed divine warnings.

Hispanoamerican written discourse of the seventeenth century offers a characteristic repertory of signs to support the main *criollo* intellectual interests of the period. Together with signs that might be called "natural"—that is, elements in Hispanoamerican reality to which the writer assigns a divine figurative function, be it as an expression of the divine presence in the New World or as a healthy moral lesson for Americans—there are also "cultural" signs obtained from the works of Peninsular writers held up as models to be followed: principally Góngora, Quevedo, Lope de Vega, and Calderón de la Barca (1600–81). In the sonnet by Fray Miguel de Guevara, *"Levántame, Señor, que estoy caído"* ["Raise me, O Lord, for I am fallen"], the reclamation of sinners is the sign that justifies the speaker's beseeching attitude. The mannerist image of the irresolute, unstable human condition is enclosed within the framework of an anguished confession of human incapacity. At the same time, the fact that others have been saved brings the speaker hope that he too, though an incorrigible sinner, can count on immanent divine forgiveness. In another of the few sonnets by Guevara that survive, the figure of Christ is a sign of divine love that places the speaker in God's everlasting debt:

Poner el Hijo en cruz, abierto el seno,
sacrificarlo porque yo no muera,
prueba es, mi Dios, de amor muy verdadera,
mostraros para mí de amor tan lleno.
Que—a ser yo Dios, y Vos hombre terreno—
os diera el ser de Dios que yo tuviera
y en el que tengo de hombre me pusiera

a trueque de gozar de un Dios tan bueno.
Y aún no era vuestro amor recompensado,
pues a mí en excelencia me habéis hecho
Dios, y a Dios al ser de hombre habéis bajado.
Deudor quedaré siempre por derecho
de la deuda que en cruz por mí ha pagado
el Hijo por dejaros satisfecho.

To place Thy Son upon the cross, His breast pierced,
to sacrifice Him so that I not die,
is proof, my Lord, of love indeed,
to show Thyself so full of love for me.
For—were I God and Thou man on earth—
I would give Thee the part of God I had,
and of that I have as man I would post
for barter for joy at having such a God.
And even if Thy love were not repaid,
in excellence Thou wouldst have made me
God, and God to being man Thou hadst come down.
Debtor I shall remain, and by right
of that debt paid for me on the cross
by Thy Son, to satisfy Thee.

In the *"Canción a la vista de un desengaño"* ["Song on Being Unde-
ceived"], by Matías de Bocanegra (Mexico, 1612–68), an attempt is
made, also from a post-Tridentine Catholic perspective, to solve the
question of free will—a problem that repeatedly recurs in baroque
interpretations of human existence. To this end the speaker uses the
mannerist image of an irresolute and anguished monk, painfully vacil-
lating about his vocation and trying to find peace of mind. He arrives
at a spring meadow of dazzling beauty, which symbolizes the glory of
life on earth. The song of a linnet supports his decision to abandon
the cloister; he reflects, "One can also be saved in the secular world."
In the lyric enunciation an unmistakable echo of *La vida es sueño* [Life
is a Dream] by Calderón can be heard when the monk considers the
paradox of his existence. Although a human being and born free, he
lives under restrictive authority, while the fish, birds, roses, and
streams enjoy the liberty of a peaceful, pleasant, harmonious life in
spite of being without free will. The monk's conclusion is quickly and

emphatically contradicted by an unexpected turn of events: the sudden death of the singing bird in the talons of a hawk is the critical episode that destroys the beautiful placid order of the meadow. The harmonious world crumbles and the false, deceptive character of things is exposed. The monk discovers with astonishment that all is appearance, that the senses can easily deceive if one only looks at the surface of objects. The beauty of the world is intrinsically dangerous because it carries within itself the germs of its own destruction.

Forced to choose between unprotected liberty and a return to a restricted home, but one that takes care of those who live within it, Bocanegra's monk decides without the slightest shadow of a doubt:

> *Si el arroyo, el pez, el ave*
> *la rosa por libres mueren*
> *en pez, en ave, en arroyo*
> *y en rosa es bien que escarmientes.*
> *Que si preso me gano,*
> *de voluntad a la prisión me allano;*
> *y si libre me pierdo,*
> *no quiero libertad tan sin acuerdo.*

> If the stream, the fish, the bird,
> the rose die because they are free,
> from the fish, the bird, the stream,
> and the rose it is good to take warning.
> If I gain from being prisoner,
> I willingly reconcile myself to prison;
> if I lose by being free,
> I do not want such disagreeable freedom.

The *"Canción"* presents a typical baroque picture of reality: human beings live within a space full of false signs surrounded by deceptive beauty, subject to the seduction of the transitory, permanently confronted with the risk of error; but God knows how to show His presence through signs that will save one from being deceived when about to fall. The apparent stability of the world is disturbed and gives way to chaos and despair, to teach us an edifying lesson. In this way the conflicts that arise in the mannerist understanding are solved in baroque literary discourse through assertive enunciations leaving no room whatsoever for doubt and indecision. Bocanegra's monk returns sadder but wiser to the religious home he was about to leave.

The baroque tendency toward representational inflation is considerably reduced in the works of Sor Juana Inés de la Cruz (Mexico, 1648–95). In general, Sor Juana's lyric poetry lacks the overemphatic grandiose style, and her aim is, rather, to internalize the aesthetic religious experience, drawing the expression of pain, disillusionment, or anxiety into her personal awareness, thus subordinating to the limits of fragile, circumscribed, individual experience the space and sense of what can be shown.

When Sor Juana's superior, the bishop of Puebla, under the pseudonym Sor Filotea, wrote criticizing her for devoting so much time to secular studies, Sor Juana, to justify the breadth and variety of her intellectual activities, replied in the *Carta a Sor Filotea* [Letter to Sister Filotea] that, as revealed by her studies, the things of this world not only do not act in conflict with each other:

> *pero se ayudan dando luz y abriendo camino las unas para las otras, por variaciones y ocultos engarces—que para esta cadena universal les puso la sabiduría de su autor—, de manera que parece se corresponden y están unidas con admirable trabazón y concierto. Es la cadena que fingieron los antiguos que salía de la boca de Júpiter, de donde pendían todas las cosas eslabonadas unas con otras. Así lo demuestra el R. P. Atanasio Quirquerio en su curioso libro De Magnete. Todas las cosas salen de Dios, que es el centro a un tiempo y la circunferencia de donde salen y donde paran todas las líneas criadas.*

but, one way or another, they help illuminate and open up the way to various and hidden connections, for they have been so placed in the universal chain by the wisdom of the author that it seems they correspond to and are united with most admirable juncture and agreement. It is this chain that the ancients used to say came from the mouth of Jupiter, and by which all things are linked together. This is what the Rev. Father Atanasio Quirquerio shows in his artful book *De Magnete*. All things come from God, who is at one and the same time the center and the circumference, from which all created lines issue and return.

For this reason, she continues:

> *Yo de mí puedo asegurar que lo que no entiendo en un autor de una facultad, lo suelo entender en otro de otra que parece muy distante; y esos propios, al explicarse, abren ejemplos metafóricos de otras artes.*

For my part, I can assure you that what I do not understand in
one author in one discipline, I understand in another from
another which seems very different; and so these in explaining
themselves open metaphorical examples of other arts.

Sor Juana's intellectual awareness derives from the integrative
cosmic design characteristic of baroque thought, but starting from that
basis, instead of projecting a vision of monumental space, restricts
itself rather to revealing the musings of an individual soul. Her lyrics
disclose a state of mind that attempts to internalize the grandiose concepts of the baroque, converting them into the silent experiences of
the private, intimate ego:

> *Amado dueño mío,*
> *escucha un rato mis cansadas quejas,*
> *pues del viento las fío,*
> *que breve las conduzca a tus orejas,*
> *si no se desvanece el triste acento*
> *como mis esperanzas en el viento.*
> *Oyeme con los ojos,*
> *ya que están tan distantes los oídos,*
> *y de ausentes enojos*
> *en ecos, de mi pluma mis gemidos;*
> *y ya que a ti no llega mi voz ruda,*
> *óyeme sordo, pues me quejo muda.*

My beloved master, listen
awhile to my weary complaints,
since I trust them to the wind
to take them quickly to your ears,
if my sad accents do not vanish
in the wind, like my hopes.
Hear me with your eyes,
for your ears are far away;
hear absent complaints
as echoes, the sighs of my pen,
and since my rude voice does not reach you,
hear me, deafly, as I mutely complain.

Sor Juana offers a vision that marks both the pinnacle and the crisis of the baroque intellectual system. Her language and modes of composition and interpretation have their roots in Góngora, Quevedo, and the great Spanish baroque writers, but reach a peak of individualized personal expression in her lyrics. The grandiose ethical spirit of the Catholic baroque is carried over into her solitary individual drama, and the desire for transcendence is considerably reduced due to her withdrawal or the failure of her impulses. Sor Juana's aesthetic awareness is not permeated by any yearning for infinity or numinous ecstasy. In her *Primero sueño* [First Dream] her soul twice fails to ascend to the First Cause. For her, the place of human beings is in this world within the compass of objects; the here and now is humanity's proper space, and to attempt to ascend is an effort frustrated by an intuitive mental incapacity natural to the human condition. In the poem the very rhythm of creation finally impedes the angry rebellious soul's renewed attempt to ascend to God.

In general, Sor Juana's lyrics look toward immediate empirical human reality and concentrate on representing the contingent. They deal with the capacities or limitations of the individual who suffers, or with successful moments of social life, and with the drama of lonely conflicts of the soul. For Sor Juana salvation does not depend so much on the individual's receiving external aid as from exercising one's own will. The recurrent motifs in the greater part of her poetry—jealousy, lack of love, remoteness, loneliness, the silence of others—do not take the form of the characteristic signs of the baroque era; they are not converted into guiding elements chosen to reveal divine management of the universal cosmic home. This explains the reduced number of signs drawn from the stereotypical repertory of literary tradition in Sor Juana's lyrics. In some of her philosophical/moral sonnets the image of the rose symbolizes the fleeting and deceptive nature of human existence, and of hope that leads to the senses being deceived; nevertheless, Sor Juana's lyrics lend renewed vigor to the baroque feeling of disenchantment. Using her own portrait as a sign, she says:

> Este que ves, engaño colorido,
> que del arte ostentando los primores,
> con falsos silogismos de colores
> es cauteloso engaño del sentido;
> éste, en quien la lisonja ha pretendido
> excusar de los años los horrores,

y venciendo del tiempo los rigores
triunfar de la vejez y del olvido,
es un vano artificio del ciudado,
es una flor al viento delicada,
es un resguardo inútil para el hado;
es una necia diligencia errada.
es un afán caduco y, bien mirado,
es cadáver, es polvo, es sombra, es nada.

This which you see, a painted lie,
boasting the beauty of art
with false syllogisms of color,
is a well-wrought deceit of the senses;
this, in which flattery attempts
to excuse the horror of the years
and defeat the severity of time,
to triumph over age and forgetfulness,
is but a vain display of artifice,
a fragile flower in the wind,
a useless precaution against fate;
a foolish, mistaken activity,
a feeble wasted effort, and, if closely viewed,
a corpse, dust, a shadow, nothingness.

The picture is a "painted lie," which tries to hide material decrepitude. In opposition to the renaissance concept of an artistic work assuming an eternal character as opposed to the transitoriness of the object depicted, here the speaker identifies the sign with the object. Everything perishes, nothing survives. Not only human beings but also their creations are subject to deterioration and destruction, as expressed in the final line on the human condition inspired by a line of Góngora.

Through elements conveying a divine message, the vital space in baroque literary work had been converted into a world of signs and symbols, illuminations, and warnings. The cosmic home had been changed into a dwelling place ruled by an inescapable system of norms whose compulsory enforcement served as protection, so that obeying the rules became a pleasant duty. Baroque representation of reality had intensified awareness of and propagandized the return to God; it defined the human being as a prodigal who has come back once again to the protective space of the home he had left behind.

The sense of religious reintegration that informs most Hispano-american baroque literature makes the moral aspects of individual and social behavior the favorite literary motifs of the period and ensures that a historical concept of artistic literary expression be viewed as a tool to further the ethical teachings of the Catholic Church. Although the baroque writers dazzle us with the linguistic innovations from Spain, seventeenth-century Hispanoamerican literary activity is best defined as writing put to doctrinal use. A good part of baroque intellectual production corresponds to this function and gives it a stamp of marked ideological severity counterbalanced by verbal brilliance of lyric expression. Along with prose discourse and seventeenth-century poetry competitions producing grandiose verse or insignificant *vers d'occasion* about everyday Hispanoamerican colonial life, we also find examples of a severe, withdrawn prose style and lyrics fulfilling a critical, moral, reformist function through bitter satire, irony, or parody.

The poetic work of Juan del Valle y Caviedes clearly expresses the bitterness of many disenchanted, skeptical seventeenth-century intellectuals. His poetry reevaluates social customs, reinterprets myths inherited from renaissance culture, and rewrites texts by prestigious authors. The everyday world and that of high culture are amalgamated into one single object and one reality, then subjected to the speaker's piercing criticism. Del Valle y Caviedes's radical skepticism acquires a positive, aggressive stamp that distances it from the work of Quevedo; his poetry offers a challenge; it is a fervent proclamation of the right of *criollos* to decodify and reconstruct.

If the poetry of del Valle y Caviedes discloses an acid interpretation counter to the establishment view, Núñez de Pineda y Bascuñán (Chile, 1607–82) gives a different one in his *Cautiverio feliz del maestre de campo general don Francisco Núñez de Pineda y Bascuñán, y razón individual de las guerras dilatadas del Reino de Chile* [The Happy Captivity of Grandmaster General Don Francisco Núñez de Pineda y Bascuñán, and a Personal Explanation for the Protracted Wars in the Kingdom of Chile]; he offers a baroque vision of reality from the perspective of a Christian rewarded for living up to ethical Counter-Reformation standards. Started in 1656 and finished about 1673, the text relates the experiences of Núñez de Pineda when he was a prisoner of the Araucan Indians between May and November 1629. As he contemplates his distant past, the author discloses that this stage of his youth was a period of trials through which he could prove his mettle, both to his own and God's satisfaction, as an unswerving servant of the Lord.

In accord with Núñez de Pineda's baroque perspective, human existence still has a clear affiliation with the medieval point of view; God has given man the opportunity to become worthy of His divine reward promised from the beginning of time. In his discourse Núñez de Pineda shows himself as a distant intellectual descendant of St. Augustine, characterized, however, in his immediate surroundings according to typical mannerist norms; he is a lonely individual, torn by the struggle between the traditional forces of the angels and those of the devil, between spiritual duties and weakness of the flesh, over which he always triumphs thanks to his profound felicitous confidence in Divine Providence. In this ceaseless struggle woman is par excellence the sign of the danger of sin. In his captivity Núñez de Pineda apparently lived under constant siege by Araucan girls, but his conduct (at least, according to his own report written long after the fact) never deviated from the strict moral code that distinguishes the good servant of God. Knightly *courtoisie* and moral firmness are the notes that always characterized his Christian behavior.

When the daughter of Cacique Ancanamón invites him seductively to dance and drink, he replies that Christians must never offend God in such a way, and much less with infidel women, since that would be a double sin. On a similar occasion he protests that his only pleasure is to fear God; another time he comes upon a group of naked Indian girls who invite him to bathe with them. The image so impressed him that, on remembering it, he says:

> *Confieso a Dios mi culpa, y al lector aseguro como humano, que no me ví jamás en mayor aprieto, tentado y perseguido del común adversario.*

> I confess my sin to God, and assure the reader as another human being that I have never found myself in a tighter spot, or been so tempted and pursued by the common enemy.

But he overcomes the Devil and "with polite thanks" to the girls declines their invitation and looks for a distant place where he can bathe alone. Recalling the occasion when he was forced to dance with the daughter of Cacique Quilalebo, he reflects:

> *Jamás me vi más atribulado ni más perseguido del demonio que en esta ocasión forzosa e inexcusable, porque era aplaudido de los caciques y solicitado con amor y voluntad a sensuales apetitos.*

I was never more troubled nor more pursued by the Devil than on this inexcusable but unavoidable occasion, when I was urged on by the applauding caciques and lovingly begged to indulge my sensual appetites.

In general, Núñez de Pineda's story of the moral dangers he ran during his captivity follows the baroque descriptive schema: temptation and resistance; risk of sin, which he exorcises, swearing fidelity to God. For this reason, in telling of his experience so many years after the event, Núñez de Pineda explains:

Doy infinitas gracias al Señor, que habiendo asistido en compañía de lasciva gente y en festejos deshonestos y torpes, solicitado de los propios caciques, agasajado de las mujeres, y aun incitado algunas veces, podré asegurar muy bien, no quiero decir que me faltasen, como a muchacho, diversos pensamientos malos e interiores tentaciones, que el más justo no está libre de ellas, que todo el tiempo que asistí cautivo entre naturales, no falté a la obligación de cristiano procurando parecerlo también en mis acciones, sin que de ellas pudiesen echar mano para calumniar nuestra religión cristiana, como lo hacían con la memoria de los sucesos pasados que adelante iremos manifestando.

I give infinite thanks to God for having helped me, being in the company of a lascivious people, with their disreputable and senseless feasting; urged on by the caciques themselves, toasted by the women, and even incited at times, I can well assure you; I do not wish to say that, as a boy [in fact, a 22-year-old man] I was lacking divers evil thoughts and inner temptations, since even the most upright man is not free from these; yet all the time I was a captive of the natives I never failed in my Christian duty, trying to appear Christian in my actions also, or else they could have slandered our religion, as they did with the memory of events of which I will speak later.

The image of the captive created by Núñez y Pineda is characterized by his absolute, indestructible belief in the divine guidance of history. If human beings are capable of overcoming the obstacles and temptations the Devil puts in their path, if they have faith and enough Christian experience to distinguish between the true and false signs that reality offers, then they will earn never-ending divine protection. Núñez de Pineda explains why Cacique Maulicán defended him from the other caciques who wished to put him to death:

Lo tercero y principal que pude colegir de la firmeza y constancia que en defenderme y ampararme tuvo el dueño de mis acciones, fue la Providencia divina, que le ponía esfuerzo y ánimo varonil para que se opusiese a las contradicciones y aprietos que le hacían, solicitándole la voluntad por todos los caminos para la consecución de mi suerte y de mi fin desastrado.

The third and chief reason that I could deduce for the firmness and constancy with which he defended and supported me was that Divine Providence, the master of my fate, put force and manly spirit into him so that he would oppose their arguments, using every means to urge benevolence to the benefit of my fortunes and my proposed wretched end.

As is logical to suppose, the baroque perspective projected by Núñez de Pineda onto the narrative of his adventures covers all the different linguistic registers that make up the discourse of the *Cautiverio feliz*. Much less space in the text is given to the narrative than to the nonnarrative parts; as happens with most of the texts whose structures maintain the polymorphism characteristic of mannerist art, critics have found *Cautiverio feliz* both interesting and confusing. The story has been defined as "history," a "tale," a "memoir," a "didactic-political treatise," an "autobiography," and even a "novel" by critics concerned with fitting particular works into a preconceived scheme of classification. Traditional critics have been in almost unanimous agreement about its lack of unity, and have therefore relegated to a position of secondary importance the very aspects that in the author's judgment take precedence in the structural hierarchy of the work. The most frequently discussed portions of the text have been the narrative ones—that is to say, the story of the protagonist's adventures among the Indians—and the voluminous nonnarrative portions have been considered "digressions," which simply add bulk and spoil the overall shape. This goes directly against Núñez de Pineda's own words, since on more than one occasion he insists that the digressions are the main purpose of the book, finally going so far as to say that the book's true intent can be found there "and not in the actual story, which I have written succinctly."

The title of the book refers then to the two levels within it: it is the story of the writer's captive life among the Araucans, and a commentary on and explanation of why the war between the Europeans and the natives in the kingdom of Chile has dragged on for so long.

The unity of the text, instead of being weakened by these apparently different aims, is confirmed through each, because the baroque perspective of the author subordinates all elements of the structure to one central organizing principle. Telling about his personal experiences serves to prove that good servants who live up to the norms of Christian doctrine always get their reward. The nonnarrative parts of the discourse, on the other hand, assert that those norms have been forgotten by the *criollos* in Chile, and this ethical deviation is denounced as the root cause of the unending struggle between the conquerors and the conquered. Both portions unite to fulfill an edifying purpose that is typically baroque: the text proposes that moral conduct in accordance with Christian ethics would be the solution to the protracted wars in the kingdom of Chile.

THE AFFIRMATION OF HISPANOAMERICAN IDENTITY

The works of the principal Hispanoamerican baroque writers brought to a close an intellectual cycle that had started with the first Gothic interpretations of the New World. The process of cosmic religious integration that these baroque works proposed, through the dialectic between hyperbole and comparison, culminated in a discourse emphatically affirming the universal, divine nature of the cosmos.

The surprise expressed by the first chroniclers, who bore witness to the world they were seeing, revealed a sense of otherness that they felt from the depths of their being, an otherness that they initially attempted to rationalize through a synthesis of the surprising natural and human geography of the recently discovered space and the medieval concept of the universe as a "good house." They tried to integrate the new with that which was already known and so overcome the feeling of discomfort hidden beneath their astonishment; as a result, utopian imagery was assimilated into notions of familiarity, and Hispanoamerica was conceived by those conquistadors who first saw it as a unique, marvelous space filled with the fantastic images of late medieval consciousness, but which also reproduced the everyday conditions of the home space left behind. It was, in short, a "fantastic everyday world," a space that allowed the marvelous and the ordinary to coexist, as unlimited liberty could also coexist there with the standards brought from home.

As the Spanish grammarian Antonio de Nebrija (1441?–1552) had foretold, language, the faithful companion of the empire, would very soon begin an intellectual journey toward a space imbued with difference. Language was obliged to abandon concepts of the known when attempting to describe unfamiliar specific defining traits of American space. The first effort at forming a new concept of American reality by the mannerists, was, nevertheless, quickly annulled by the early imposition in Hispanoamerica of the post-Tridentine baroque integrative and conservative outlook. Baroque writing insisted on the radical continuity of the premannerist, even prerenaissance, concept of existence and emphasized belief in an integral cosmic unity in which all spaces are as one under the omnipresent gaze of their Creator. In this way another attempt was made to equate the Hispanoamerican world with the original space of the conquistadors, inasmuch as both constituted a cosmic unity whose meaning and reason for being were part of God's historical design. The universe had a divine spiritual unity in which differences were erased and distances integrated, a space of infinite correlations that caused an ecstatic thrill in those who contemplated it. America was simply one element, one piece within the continuous mechanism leading straight to the First Cause. The uniquely American features of the New World were, for some baroque thinkers, merely variants of God's universal schema of history: the Aztec gods were identified with pagan and Christian deities, and Biblical images were projected onto the American landscape.

The effort at integration that Hispanoamerican baroque writers carried out led to widely different conclusions. In their enthusiasm to demonstrate America's similarity with the rest of the divine cosmos and its important participation in the divine design that upheld it, these writers were the first to pay any real attention to American physical surroundings and to express authentic interest in whatever it offered that was original and new. Their need to assimilate had the effect of leading them once again to note the "difference," and so, paradoxically, we have the second definitive "discovery" of American space.

Padre José de Acosta, for example, in spite of his integrationist and universalist philosophy, had no other option but to oppose, with irony, those intellectuals who struggled to fit new American discoveries into the European frame of reality. His irony is clear proof that he too recognized the different, individual nature of the New World. On speaking of American fauna unknown in Europe, he says:

> quien por esta vía de poner sólo diferencias accidentales pretendiere salvar la propagación de los animales de Indias y reducirlos a las de

Europa, tomará carga, que mal podrá salir con ella. Porque si hemos de juzgar de las especies de los animales por sus propiedades, son tan diversas que quererlas reducir a especies conocidas de Europa, será llamar al huevo castaña.

whoever by these means says the differences are accidental and attempts to explain the propagation of animals in the Indies by limiting them to those found in Europe, will be biting off more than he can chew. For we must study species of animals by the properties they possess; they are so diverse that to try to reduce them all to species known in Europe will be calling an egg an oyster. [Historia, III, xxxvi]

The first awakening of real awareness of America had been seen, it is true, in the work of those figures representative of the mannerist outlook, but the results had been relative. Disjunction between interior and exterior, between immediate, surrounding physical space and imaginary or remembered space, between "ours" and "theirs," was blunted in these writers, blocked by oblique viewpoints, rhetorical language, idealization, systems of interpretation, or representational codes still too closely tied to European roots. Mariano Latorre in 1944 bitterly reproached Ercilla for his lack of interest in the Chilean landscape—an unjust criticism, since Ercilla was not of the intellectual disposition to notice his immediate surroundings, or the patterned skin markings of the aborigines, however much he admired the people. Both dimensions of reality were simply variants for Ercilla, particular forms of the universal humanist principle he was defending. The Inca Garcilaso, for his part, in order to gain historical recognition for the kingdom of his forebears, presented a favorable utopian vision of them in which the Incaic was assimilated into the European, causing him to contradict the very idea of "difference," which had impelled him to write his work. The deeply felt, painful sorrow with which he looked at the Inca past was, in fact, the very obstacle that got in the way of his seeing it.

Awareness of American difference tended to disappear almost as soon as it appeared. If it is true that Bernardo de Balbuena was the first poet in Hispanoamerican literature to write a panegyric to a city, the purpose of his praise was to subordinate Mexico to Spain. Even though the artful shepherds of *Los sirgueros de la Virgen* have left Arcady to move around in a decidedly Mexican world, the spirit in Bramón's work transcends the local color of the writing and relates it, anachronistically, to a foreign literary model, while it is silent about the existential problems of *criollo* society in America.

Seventeenth-century baroque writing had as its starting point the intellectual paradox mentioned above. This defined the American world according to a specific concept, with an aim to assimilate and a goal to reaccommodate a divine system of interpretation; recognition of a system of intrinsic values in the Hispanoamerican world was a prerequisite. A critical, vigilant attitude had to be maintained in order to reinforce the established norms that now officially regulated reality. Starting with the generation of Alonso de Ovalle (1600–51), a spirit of polemics and debate, which the work of the seventeenth-century eye-witness chronicles had revealed, began to rise again, culminating with the great figures of the Hispanoamerican late baroque: Sor Juana, Sigüenza y Góngora, "El Lunarejo" (Espinosa Medrano), and del Valle y Caviedes.

Ovalle's integrationalist attitudes grow pale in the total context of his work, especially where we see him identify with his American surroundings; his writing is filled with unmistakable notes of joy and pleasure. Ruiz de Alarcón (Mexico, 1580–Spain, 1639), writing in Spain, viewed the social world of Madrid with the eyes of a "colonial," an outsider whose sense of otherness allowed him to see through and analyze the social world around him. Núñez de Pineda's criticism of those who stray from the path of Christian ethics laid open to discourse a proposed new schema of conduct, since, although the European model was adhered to, he stressed that we should always take into consideration the particularities of the space in which the conduct was to be put into practice. At the same time, the disenchanted vision of the narrator of *Infortunios de Alonso Ramírez*, the doubt implicit in *Primero sueño*, the sarcastic criticism of del Valle y Caviedes's *Diente del Parnaso* [The Bite of Parnassus], and the polemical attitude of Espinosa Medrano's *Apologético en favor de don Luis de Góngora* were all signs in the second half of the seventeenth century that a crisis was occurring in baroque thought as originally conceived. This crisis not only marked the imminent decline of an interpretive system that had begun to be questioned by Hispanoamerican intellectuals, but also signaled the rise of awareness of Hispanoamerica's own individual space, its own differentiated, cosmic "good house." The new way of interpreting reality had been generated by a system of thought brought from abroad, but at the same time persevered in trying to establish a code of conduct arising from a synthesis of what had been assimilated and criticism of it.

Awareness that a new note had been struck is unequivocally revealed in the tone of intellectual pride that appears in Sigüenza y
Góngora's scientific writings, in the cruel mockery that del Valle y
Caviedes directs at the medical ignorance of his time, in Espinosa
Medrano's defense of the right of Americans to argue with Europeans,
in Sor Juana's verses on the rights of women in society and the irony
with which she describes in an *ovillejo* (a verse form) the worn out
baroque language used by the poets of her time:

> *Y así andan los poetas desvalidos,*
> *achicando antiguallas de vestidos;*
> *y tal vez, sin mancilla,*
> *lo que es jubón, ajustan a ropilla,*
> *o hacen de unos centones*
> *de remiendos diversos, los calzones;*
> *y nos quieren vender por extremada,*
> *una belleza rota y remendada.*
> *¿Pues qué es ver las metáforas cansadas*
> *en que han dado las Musas alcanzadas?*
> *No hay ciencia, arte, ni oficio,*
> *que con extraño vicio*
> *los poetas, con vana sutileza,*
> *no anden acomodando a la belleza;*
> *y pensando que pintan de los cielos,*
> *hacen unos retablos de sus duelos.*

And so they go, the helpless poets,
cutting down old-fashioned garments;
what was a doublet will make a jacket,
perhaps without a single blemish;
cut one piece into a hundred
patches for repairing breeches;
they want to sell us as finished product
one torn beauty and a repaired one.
What's to see in worn out metaphors
discarded even by the Muses?
There is no science, art, employment,
that poets with their strange vice

and vain subtlety,
have not tried to pass as beauty,
and thinking that they paint heaven,
make altarpieces of their efforts.

Wylie Sypher defined the baroque as art for solving problems. It tried to solve the unresolved metaphysical doubts and social unrest that shows through mannerist art. This problem-solving function of the baroque appeared very early in Hispanoamerica and was strengthened by the work of writers during the seventeenth century. But, as we have seen, along the way to reintegration, the spatial difference emerged once again. Contradicting their own efforts at assimilation, Hispanoamerican writers, in a repertoire of varied texts, reveal only distance, separation, criticism, and will to difference—that is to say, awareness of their own separate reality—and the concept of feeling placed, after all, in a space that, however unstable and contradictory, is the place where they truly belong.

On studying the works of the four authors named above, the Cuban critic, José Juan Arrom, established that the characteristic notes for all of them are a polemical and rebellious attitude toward the establishment, an effort to synthesize the American and European, and a defiant will to know—a trait in which, significantly, the three *criollos* differ from del Valle y Caviedes, the only writer of the four who was born in Spain. If the work of these four marks the peak of the baroque style in colonial Hispanoamerica, as has been said, or, if on the contrary it represents the decline of this style, as other critics believe, it in no way weakens their attitude vis-à-vis their surroundings: a passionate defense of American intellectual identity and the right to sincere, honest searching while voicing its differences from its Peninsular origins. As regards those differences, the textual dialog with Spanish literature produced in America should not be viewed lightly: Sor Juana reorganized the dramatic elements of Calderón and imitated Góngora's style but created a world of her own; del Valle y Caviedes rewrote Segismundo's monologue from Calderón's *La vida es sueño*; Sigüenza y Góngora Americanized an imported culture. At first glance, they may appear to have simply imitated prestigious models, but what has been done, on the contrary, is to reinforce a sense of difference, motivated by intertextual activity. By rewriting and incorporating other texts, they changed, transformed, and emphasized the importance that distance and difference of identity conferred, lending strength to Sigüenza y Góngora's demand that Europeans respect the intellectual stature of the Americans. In the words of that Mexican thinker we find all the pride of being in a New World that had found its place, of being in the home where one belongs, within humanity's cosmic space.

REFERENCES

This study represents a synthesis of readings that have taken place over several years and, consequently, can provide only a hint of the many concepts that have contributed to its content. I have preferred, therefore, to name below such texts as I recall having proved fruitful, and to which I owe, to a greater or lesser degree, the ideas formulated in the preceding pages. Some references published after 1987 have been added to this edition to provide the reader with up-to-date information.

—José Promis

For the convenience of the readers of this English translation, versions available in English, and sometimes later editions than those originally cited by the author, have been substituted when they have come to our attention.

—Alita Kelley and Alec E. Kelley

Acosta, Leonardo. "El barroco hispanoamericano y la ideología colonista," in *Unión*. 1972.

Alegría, Fernando. *La poesía chilena. Orígenes y desarrollo del siglo XVI al XIX.* 1954.

Anadón, José. *Pineda y Bascuñán, defensor del araucano.* 1977.

Anderson Imbert, Enrique. "La forma autor-personaje en una novela mexicana del siglo XVII," in his *Crítica interna.* 1961.

———. *Spanish-American Literature. A History.* 1963.

Antelo, Antonio. "Literatura y sociedad en la América española del siglo XVII: notas para su estudio," in *Thesaurus.* 1973.

Arce de Vásquez, Margot. *Garcilaso de la Vega: contribución al estudio de la lírica española del siglo XVI,* 2nd ed. 1961.

Arocena, Luis. *El inca Garcilaso y el humanismo renacentista*. 1949.
Arrom, José Juan. *Esquema generacional de las letras hispanoamericanas*. 1977.
Auerbach, Erich. *Mimesis. The Representation of Reality in Western Literature*. 1953.
Avalle-Arce, Juan Bautista. *El inca Garcilaso en sus "Comentarios."* 1944.
————. "El poeta en su poema (El caso Ercilla)," in *Revista de Occidente*. 1971.
Bataillon, Marcel. *Erasmo y España*. 1950.
Beverly, John. "On Góngora and colonial Góngorism," in *Revista Iberoamericana*. 1981.
Burckhardt, Jacob. *The Civilization of the Renaissance in Italy*. 1961.
Carilla, Emilio. *El barroco literario hispánico*. 1969.
————. *El gongorismo en América*. 1946.
————. *La literatura barroca en Hispanoamérica*. 1972.
————. "Literatura barroca y ámbito colonial," in *Thesaurus*. 1969.
Castagnino, Raúl H. "Carlos de Sigüenza y Góngora o la picaresca a la inversa," in *Razón y Fábula*. 1971.
Castro, Américo. *La realidad histórica de España*, 3rd ed., rev. 1966.
Chang-Rodríguez, Raquel. "Apuntes sobre sociedad y literatura hispanoamericana del siglo XVII," in *Cuadernos Americanos*. 1974.
————. "El prólogo al lector en *El carnero*: guía para su lectura," in *Thesaurus*. 1974.
Concha, Jaime. "La literatura colonial hispanoamericana: Problemas e hipótesis," in *Neohelicon*. 1976.
————. "El otro Nuevo Mundo," in *Homenaje a Ercilla*. 1969.
Correa Bello, Sergio. *El cautiverio feliz en la vida política chilena del siglo XVII*. 1965.
Cueva, Agustín. "El espejismo heroico de la Conquista (Ensayo de interpretación de *La Araucana*)," in *Casa de las Américas*. 1978.
Curtius, Ernst Robert. *European Literature and the Latin Middle Ages*. 1973.
Díaz-Plaja, Guillermo. *El espíritu del barroco*. 1940.
Durán Luzio, Juan. "Hacia los orígenes de una literatura colonial," in *Revista Iberoamericana*. 1974.
Esteve Barba, Francisco. *Historiografía indiana*. 1964.
Frankl, Víctor. *El "Antijovio" de Gonzalo Jiménez de Quesada y las concepciones de realidad y verdad en la época de la contrarreforma y el manierismo*. 1963.
Fuentes, Carlos. *Cervantes o la crítica de la lectura*. 1976.
Goić, Cedomil. *Historia y Crítica de la Literatura Hispanoamericana. 1. Epoca Colonial*. 1988.
————. "La periodisation dans l'histoire de la littérature hispanoaméricaine," in *Etudes littéraires*. 1975.
————. "Poética del exordio en *La Araucana*," in *Revista Chilena de Literatura*. 1970.
————. "La tópica de la conclusión en Ercilla," in *Revista Chilena de Literatura*. 1971.
Hatzfeld, Helmut. *Estudios sobre el barroco*. 1964.
Hauser, Arnold. *Mannerism: The Crisis of the Renaissance and the Origin of Modern Art*. 1965.

———. *The Social History of Art*. 1957–58.

Henríquez Ureña, Pedro. *A Concise History of Latin American Culture*. 1966.

———. *Literary Currents in Hispanic America*. 1945.

———. *Seis ensayos en busca de nuestra expresión*. 1952.

Hernández Sánchez-Barba, Mario. *Historia y literatura en Hispanoamérica (1492–1820)*. 1978.

Huizinga, Johan. *The Waning of the Middle Ages*. 1924.

Iñigo Madrigal, Luis, ed. *Historia de la literatura hispanoamericana. Tomo I. Epoca Colonial*. 1982.

Iventosch, Herman. *Los nombres bucólicos en Sannazaro y la pastoral española*. 1975.

Lafuente Ferrari, Enrique. "La interpretación del Barroco y sus valores españoles," in Werner Weisbach, *El Barroco, arte de la contrarreforma*. 1948.

Lagmanovich, David. "Para una caracterización de *Infortunios de Alonso Ramírez*," in *Sin Nombre*. 1974.

Latorre, Mariano. *La literatura de Chile*. 1944.

Leal, Luis. "El *Cautiverio feliz* y la crónica novelesca," in *Prosa hispanoamericana virreinal* (ed. Raquel Chang-Rodríguez). 1978.

Leonard, Irving. *Books of the Brave: Being an Account of Books and of Men in the Spanish Conquest and Settlement of the Sixteenth-Century New World*. 1949.

———. *Don Carlos de Sigüenza y Góngora, a Mexican Savant of the Seventeenth Century*. 1929.

Lida de Malkel, María Rosa. *La idea de la fama en la Edad Media castellana*. 1952.

Loveluck, Juan. "En indio en *La Araucana* y en las literaturas de Hispanoamérica" (introduction to *La Araucana*, Santiago, Zig-Zag). 1974.

Lukács, Georgy. *The Historical Novel*. 1962.

———. *Theory of the Novel*. 1971.

Maravall, José Antonio. *Culture of the Baroque: Analysis of a Historical Structure*. 1986.

Martinengo, Alessandro. "La cultura literaria de Juan Rodríguez Freile," in *Thesaurus*. 1964.

Méndez Plancarte, Alfonso. *Poetas novohispanos*. 1942–45.

Montesinos, José F. *Introducción a una historia de la novela en España en el siglo XIX*. 1955.

Morínigo, Marcos A., and Isaías Lerner. Introduction in *La Araucana* (Madrid, Castalia). 1979.

Parra Sandoval, Rodrigo. "El intelectual de la Colonia: *El carnero* como una visión de mundo," in *Razón y Fábula*. 1973.

Pascual Buxó, José. "Bernardo de Balbuena y el manierismo novohispano," in *Studi Ispanici*. 1977.

Pastor, Beatriz. *Discursos narrativos de la conquista: mitificación y emergencia*. 1983.

Picón-Salas, Mariano. *A Cultural History of Spanish America, from Conquest to Independence*. 1962.

Pupo-Walker, Enrique. "Los *Comentarios reales* y la historicidad de lo imaginario," in *Revista Iberoamericana*. 1978.

———. "Sobre el discurso narrativo y sus referentes en los *Comentarios reales* del inca Garcilaso de la Vega," in *Prosa Hispanoamericana virreinal*. 1978.

Reyes, Alfonso. *Letras de la Nueva España*. 1944.

Reynolds, Winston A. *Espiritualidad de la conquista de México. Su perspectiva religiosa en las letras de la Edad de Oro*. 1966.

Rodríguez Marín, Francisco. *El "Quijote" y Don Quijote en América*. 1911.

Rodríguez Moñino, Antonio. "Sobre poetas hispanoamericanos de la época virreinal," in *Papeles de Son Armadans*. 1968.

Roggiano, Alfredo. "Acerca de los dos barrocos: el de España y el de América," in *Memoria del XVII Congreso del Instituto Internacional de Literatura Iberoamericana*. 1975.

Rosenblat, Angel. *La primera visión de América y otros estudios*. 1965.

Sánchez, Luis Alberto. *Escritores representativos de América*, 2nd ed. 1963.

———. *Los poetas de la Colonia y de la revolución*. 1974.

Spingarn, Joel Elias. *A History of Literary Criticism in the Renaissance*, 2nd ed., rev. 1908.

Sypher, Wylie. *Four Stages of Renaissance Style: Transformations in Art and Literature, 1400–1700*. 1978.

Todorov, Tzvetan. *La Conquista de América. La cuestión del otro*. 1987.

Triviños, Gilverto. "Bernardo del Carpio desencantado por Barnardo de Balbuena," in *Revista Chilena de Literatura*. 1980–81.

Van Horne, John. *Bernardo de Balbuena. Biografía y crítica*. 1972.

Vidal, Hernán. *Socio-historia de la literatura colonial hispanoamericana: tres lecturas orgánicas*. 1985.

Von Martin, Alfred. *Sociología del Renacimiento*. 1966.

Weisbach, Werner. *El Barroco, arte de la contrarreforma*. 1948.

Wölfflin, Heinrich. *Principles of Art History*. 1950, reprint of 7th ed. 1932.

Zavala, Silvio. *La filosofía política en la conquista de América*. 1947.

Zea, Leopoldo. *The Latin-American Mind*. 1970.

INDEX OF PERSONS
AND LITERARY WORKS